Erich Fromm

Rainer Funk

Erich Fromm
His Life and Ideas

An Illustrated Biography

Translated by
Ian Portman and Manuela Kunkel

CONTINUUM

NEW YORK • LONDON

2000

The Continuum International Publishing Group Inc
370 Lexington Avenue, New York, NY 10017

The Continuum International Publishing Group Ltd
Wellington House, 125 The Strand, London WC2R 0BB

This translation has been supported by Ingeborg Teek Frank.

Printed in the United States of America

Library of Congress Cataloging in Publication Data

Funk, Rainer
  [Erich Fromm. English]
  Erich Fromm: his life and ideas : an illustrated biography /
  Rainer Funk; translated by Ian Portman and Manuela Kunkel
     p. cm.

  Includes bibliographical references (p.) and index.
  ISBN 0-8264-1224-6 (hardcover)
  1. Fromm, Erich, 1900- 2. Psychoanalysts–United States–Biography.
  I. Title.

  BF109.F76 F8413 2000
  150.19'57'092–dc21
  [B]   00-021987

Contents

1
A Background of Tradition: Family and Childhood

"For me modern life was really not quite understandable; I didn't understand why people lived that way; I felt sorry for them. So, my spiritual home was–one has to say–a medieval atmosphere, in which everything was directed to traditional learning, to the perfection of man, to spiritual values; and while I went to a German school and took part in German culture as every other boy or student did who lived in Germany, I was a stranger–very definitely so–and I indeed never regretted that."[1]

These words of the eighty-year-old Erich Fromm, taken from an interview with Gerard Khoury, reflect the productive tensions which determined the great psychoanalyst's life from the beginning.

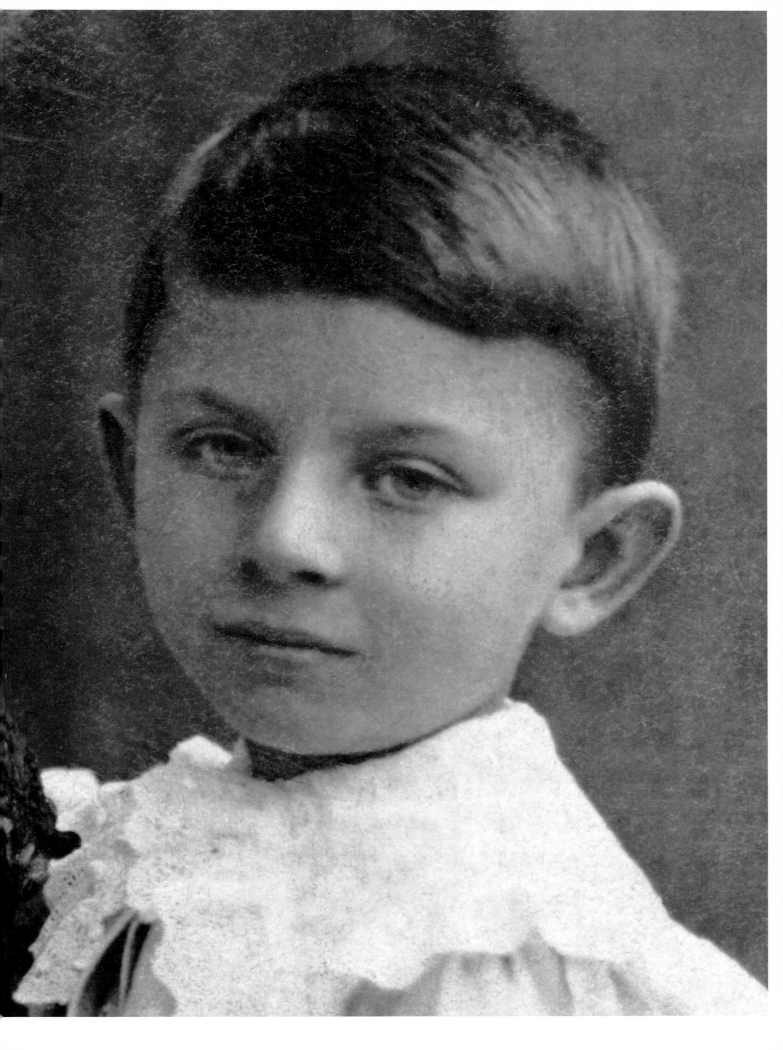

Erich Fromm grew up on the first floor of the house at 27 Liebigstrasse in the west of Frankfurt.

He received his first lessons in the Talmud from Ludwig Krause, his great uncle on his mother's side. The famous Talmudist from Posen spend his later years in the Fromm household in Frankfurt.

The Orthodox Jewish background in which Erich Fromm grew up differed markedly from the bourgeois-liberal spirit of Frankfurt at the beginning of the twentieth century. Far from suffering from this, however, the young Fromm was spurred on to self-confidence and the discovery of his own identity.

Fromm often referred to the "medieval atmosphere" in which he spent his childhood. Even after he rejected Orthodox Judaism at the age of twenty-six, he continued to identify throughout his life with this atmosphere. What did it mean to him?

"I found it as a child very strange that people devote their life to making money and I was very embarrassed when a man had to admit in my presence that he was a businessman; in other words, that he spent his whole time making money! I felt ashamed for him, that he was forced to make that admission! In that sense I was really not born in the modern era, because I just couldn't understand a world in which making money was or should be the main occupation of people."[1]

In the world that Fromm knew as a child, studying was the main occupation–the study of the religious scriptures of Judaism. For a long time he hoped to make the study of the Talmud his life's work, in accordance with a tradition from both sides of his family. But for Fromm, the main point was, perhaps, not what he studied, but rather the values attached to studying and the different way of life that marks it out.

To illustrate the significance of study of the Talmud, Fromm liked to relate an incident, that was told of his great-grandfather, the rabbi Seligmann Bär Bamberger, known as the "Würzburger Raw" (rabbi). "My great-grandfather was one of the most famous Jewish scholars. He had, as was customary in that time, a small shop in Wiesenbronn (near Würzburg) in which he spent most of his time studying the Talmud. When a client came in he became angry and said 'Is there no other shop than mine? As you can see I am busy.'" [2]

When not engaged in studying in his shop, his great-grandfather–the most important figure of Orthodox Jewry in south Germany in the nineteenth century–taught in the Jüdische Lehrerbildungsanstalt (Jewish Teacher-Training Institute) that he had founded in Würzburg.

Of course, this prebourgeois, "medieval" world of his great-grandfather was not the only one in which Erich Fromm grew up.

Erich Fromm with his great-uncle Ludwig Krause, studying the Talmud. "One time I asked him–I knew he liked me–'Uncle what do you think will become of me?' hoping he would say something nice. He said: 'An old Jew!' That was a very characteristic Jewish answer to discourage any kind of ambition."[1]

Although there are no photographs of Fromm's great-grandfather, Seligmann Bär Bamberger (the "Würzburger Raw") and his wife Kela, their gravestones in the Jewish cemetery at Höchberg near Würzburg survive.

In 1852, the eldest daughter of the "Würzburger Raw," Rahel Bamberger (right) married one of her father's students, Rabbi Seligmann Pinchas Fromm—grandfather of Erich Pinchas Fromm. He started his career as rabbi of the county of Bad Homburg vor der Höhe (near Frankfurt), later, in 1875, becoming house rabbi of Baron Willi Carl von Rothschild in Frankfurt.

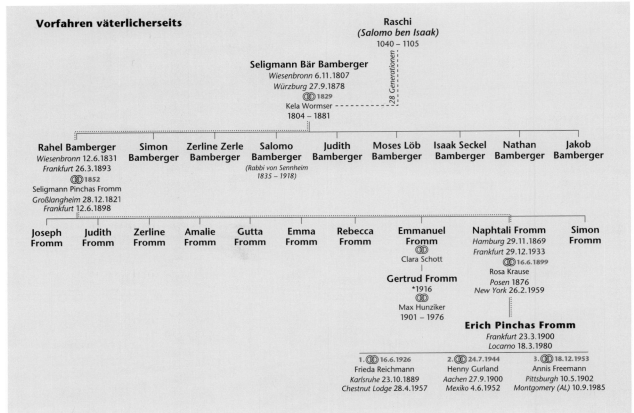

Vorfahren väterlicherseits

Raschi
(Salomo ben Isaak)
1040 – 1105

Seligmann Bär Bamberger
Wiesenbronn 6.11.1807
Würzburg 27.9.1878
⚭ 1829
Kela Wormser
1804 – 1881

28 Generationen

| Rahel Bamberger | Simon Bamberger | Zerline Zerle Bamberger | Salomo Bamberger | Judith Bamberger | Moses Löb Bamberger | Isaak Seckel Bamberger | Nathan Bamberger | Jakob Bamberger |

Rahel Bamberger
Wiesenbronn 12.6.1831
Frankfurt 26.3.1893
⚭ 1852
Seligmann Pinchas Fromm
Großlangheim 28.12.1821
Frankfurt 12.6.1898

Salomo Bamberger
(Rabbi von Sennheim 1835 – 1918)

| Joseph Fromm | Judith Fromm | Zerline Fromm | Amalie Fromm | Gutta Fromm | Emma Fromm | Rebecca Fromm | Emmanuel Fromm | Naphtali Fromm | Simon Fromm |

Emmanuel Fromm
⚭
Clara Schott

Naphtali Fromm
Hamburg 29.11.1869
Frankfurt 29.12.1933
⚭ 16.6.1899
Rosa Krause
Posen 1876
New York 26.2.1959

Gertrud Fromm
*1916
⚭
Max Hunziker
1901 – 1976

Erich Pinchas Fromm
Frankfurt 23.3.1900
Locarno 18.3.1980

1. ⚭ 16.6.1926
Frieda Reichmann
Karlsruhe 23.10.1889
Chestnut Lodge 28.4.1957

2. ⚭ 24.7.1944
Henny Gurland
Aachen 27.9.1900
Mexiko 4.6.1952

3. ⚭ 18.12.1953
Annis Freemann
Pittsburgh 10.5.1902
Montgomery (AL) 10.9.1985

"I was exposed to the same influences as every other young German during this time. But I had to deal with them in my own way. Not only because one always had an exceptional–not necessarily unpleasant–position as a Jew in Germany but also because I felt quite at home neither in the world I lived in, nor in the old world of traditions."[3]

The tension between these two worlds was also reflected in the profession of his father. Naphtali Fromm was first among the men on his father's side of the family not to devote himself professionally as a rabbi to the study of Jewish scripture. He was a wine merchant. Although not a scholar, his father preferred to work in the conservative Jewish community in the west of Frankfurt.

Father Naphtali Fromm and son Erich at the end of December 1913 in Montreux. "My father had a wine business; in fact he was ashamed to be a businessman. I always noticed, when friends of his ordered something from him, he felt very uncomfortable; he really wanted to separate his shameful existence as a businessman from his personal life."[1]

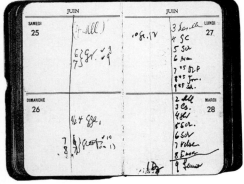

"I have had a principle all my life that I didn't analyse anybody before two o'clock in the afternoon."[1]

A page out of Fromm's diary for 1955 with a list of his Mexican patients.

Contrary to the cliché of the canny Jew, the Fromm family tradition valued study above moneymaking. Study with great-uncle Krause was followed by a period with Rabbi Nobel in Frankfurt and work on the Talmud with a private teacher, Dr. Salman Baruch Rabinkow, who came from a Hasidic background in Heidelberg.

Even after Fromm gave up the study of the Talmud for that of people's minds, and began to read widely in various scientific disciplines, he applied the rule that study had priority over earning money: "The most important thing is that I always reserved the mornings for theoretical work–and therefore kept the rule: no moneymaking things in the morning."[2]

It is not by chance that the shaping of Erich Fromm by this special world of traditional Judaism stands at the beginning of this outline of his life. Whoever knew

Erich Fromm later personally felt something of this different attitude toward reality, of a different interest in life and human beings, of his different values and the way of life that it determined.

Fromm was aware of this: "I am still an alien within the business and bourgeois cultures and this is an important reason why my attitude toward bourgeois society and capitalism has become extremely critical. I have become a socialist."[4]

Rosa Krause and Naphtali
Fromm, the parents of
Erich Fromm, were
married in 1899.

Although this Orthodox Jewish way of life formed the
basis of Erich Fromm's personality, his relationship to
and experiences with his parents and others close to
him, his school and religious education, as well as
World War I naturally contributed to the formation of
his character.

His parents, Naphtali Fromm and Rosa Krause,
married on the sixteenth of June, 1899 in Frankfurt
where, some nine months later, Erich Fromm was born
at 7.30 p.m. on the 23rd of March 1900. For a second
name he was given that of his grandfather on his
father's side–Seligmann Pinchas Fromm, although the
registry office in Frankfurt does not record him as
Erich Pinchas Fromm, but as Erich Seligmann Fromm.
Also his parents addressed his mail to "Erich S.
Fromm."

Erich Fromm remained the only child of his parents,
but there was plenty of contact with his extended
family. His father was the ninth of ten children, most of
whom were in or around Frankfurt. Six of Erich's aunts
lived in Bad Homburg vor der Höhe. Contacts to
relations on his mother's side were, however, warmer
and more frequent.

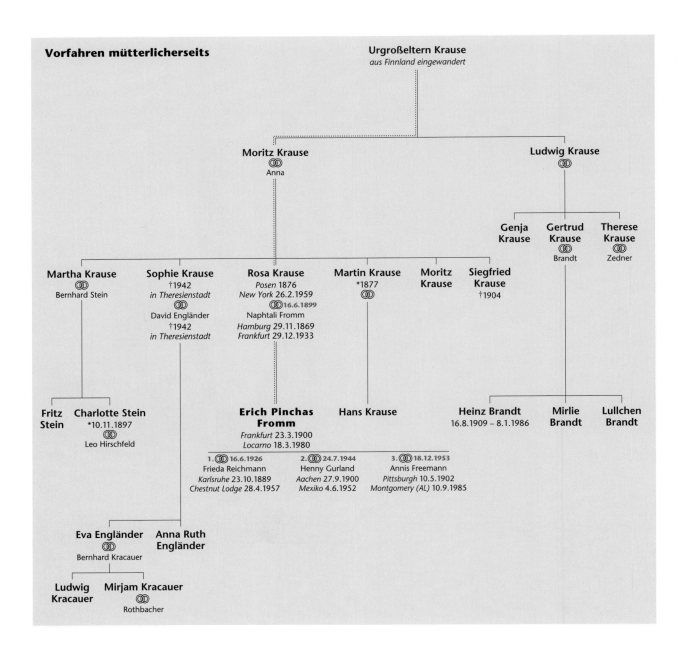

Vorfahren mütterlicherseits

Urgroßeltern Krause
aus Finnland eingewandert

Moritz Krause
⚭
Anna

Ludwig Krause
⚭

Genja Krause | **Gertrud Krause** ⚭ Brandt | **Therese Krause** ⚭ Zedner

Martha Krause
⚭
Bernhard Stein

Sophie Krause
†1942
in Theresienstadt
⚭
David Engländer
†1942
in Theresienstadt

Rosa Krause
Posen 1876
New York 26.2.1959
⚭ 16.6.1899
Naphtali Fromm
Hamburg 29.11.1869
Frankfurt 29.12.1933

Martin Krause
*1877
⚭

Moritz Krause

Siegfried Krause
†1904

Fritz Stein

Charlotte Stein
*10.11.1897
⚭
Leo Hirschfeld

Erich Pinchas Fromm
Frankfurt 23.3.1900
Locarno 18.3.1980

Hans Krause

Heinz Brandt
16.8.1909 – 8.1.1986

Mirlie Brandt

Lullchen Brandt

1. ⚭ 16.6.1926
Frieda Reichmann
Karlsruhe 23.10.1889
Chestnut Lodge 28.4.1957

2. ⚭ 24.7.1944
Henny Gurland
Aachen 27.9.1900
Mexiko 4.6.1952

3. ⚭ 18.12.1953
Annis Freemann
Pittsburgh 10.5.1902
Montgomery (AL) 10.9.1985

Eva Engländer
⚭
Bernhard Kracauer

Anna Ruth Engländer

Ludwig Kracauer

Mirjam Kracauer
⚭
Rothbacher

The Krause family came through Finland to Posen (in today's Poland), where his grandfather on his mother's side ran a cigar factory and where his brother, Dajan Ludwig Krause, became a famous scholar at the Talmudic school. (His great-uncle later came to Frankfurt and was Erich Fromm's first instructor in the Talmud.)

Moritz and Anna Krause, the maternal grand-parents of Erich Fromm.

This photograph shows Anna Krause, later to become Fromm's maternal grandmother with her six children, shortly after the early death of his grand-father, Moritz Krause. Standing behind Anna Krause is her eldest daughter Martha; to the right of her, Sophie; on the right, kneeling, is Rosa, mother of Erich Fromm; standing far left, Martin. In the fore-ground, seated, is Moritz. Siegfried, the youngest, is sitting on the table.

14

Erich Fromm's father, nicknamed "Neph," as a young man and as a father. The second photograph was taken when Erich Fromm was five years old.

Although he was often in contact with his extended family, Fromm grew up as an only child–"which is really bad."[3] Later, as a psychoanalyst, Fromm was more troubled by the neurotic influence of his parents. In a short autobiographical note in *Beyond the Chains of Illusion* (1962) he describes his father as "anxious and moody" and his mother as "prone to depression."[5]

He came to the point in an interview he gave shortly before his death. In old age he was able to see the burden of having been brought up "by two very neurotic and anxious parents"[3] in a more positive light: "Having grown up in a very neurotic family" allowed him to become "more aware of what the irrationalities of human behavior really represent."[2]

Again and again he stressed how inferior his father must have felt. Almost at the end of a row of siblings, his father was flanked by two brothers, both academics–one a doctor and one a lawyer. He probably wanted to become a rabbi. But instead he followed in the footsteps of his eldest brother and became a wine merchant. Religious tradition prevented him, however, from becoming a successful businessman. He loved religious music, had a comprehensive religious education and engaged himself successfully in the orthodox community of Frankfurt.

This photo was taken during the summer holidays at a photographers in (Bad) Herrenalb in the north of the Black Forest, and sent as a postcard on the thirty-first of July, 1911, by father and son to Erich Fromm's great-uncle Ludwig Krause at Unterberg, Moschin (close to Posen).

In his memory, Fromm experienced his father as "very neurotic, obsessive, anxious"[2]: "I suffered under the influence of a pathologically anxious father who overwhelmed me with his anxiety, at the same time not giving me any guidelines and having no positive influence on my education. He did not teach me anything; he was not interested in my personal development."[1] For fear the boy might catch a cold, he was not allowed to leave the house. He was unable to fulfil his wish to study the Talmud at the university of Lithuania for fear of hurting his father. "If my Talmudic studies would have left me in Frankfurt they wouldn't have opposed; it was the radicalism of going to Lithuania, far away, which was unacceptable."[1]
And in 1922, when Fromm completed and passed his viva: "I remember the day in 1922 I was passing all my doctoral examinations in Heidelberg, my father, who transferred his strong inferiority feeling about himself, came to Heidelberg because he was afraid I would be not received and that I might commit suicide!"[1]

Photographs of his father, especially those taken with Erich, often show an insecure and anxious man, hiding his sense of inferiority and weakness behind a stiff, correct manner. Sometimes, however, they reveal a warm and affectionate person. Even as an adolescent, Erich still enjoyed physical contact with his father, occasionally sitting on his lap.

With hindsight, Fromm saw specifically neurotic aspects in his relationship with his father. First of all: "I always felt I was the defender of my mother, who used to cry a lot and I felt I had to defend her against my father. That's the case with many boys. Later on I saw the picture was not as it first appeared. I was very fond of him and he was very fond of me. He had no fears about himself but had a neurotic anxiety about me and, as an only child, it was a very bad situation. He pampered me and I got very little discipline. He would have preferred if I had always remained a baby of three! The older I grew, the less he was interested in me, but I wouldn't say he liked me he liked me as a little baby but he was jealous of all the friends I had."[1]

Apparently Fromm senior feared his own feelings of masculine aggression and projected them onto his son. Thus he experienced his repressed aggression as fear for his son whenever Erich dared to be older than three. But when Erich chose to sit on his father's lap they became one again and the tender familiarity between the toddler and his papa was reawakened.

Another side of Erich.

The son behind the seated father. This photograph was the one by which Erich Fromm most liked to remember his father.

Erich's wish for a father who was interested in his son's development as an independent individual was disappointed. This disappointment lay behind the psychoanalyst's later ambivalence toward his father and explains his lifelong sensitivity toward those secular and religious authorities whose real interests do not lie in the autonomy and freedom of the individual.

For a brief period only, Erich found a fatherly friend who was interested in his development. When the boy was twelve years old, Oswald Sussmann, a Galician Jew employed in his father's shop, came to stay at the Fromms for two years. He introduced Erich to socialist ideas, took him for the first time to the Frankfurt Museum and took him seriously when talking politics. "He was an extremely honest man, courageous, a man of great integrity. I owe a great deal to him."[1] Sussmann was conscripted in 1914. The search for other father figures continued.

His relationship with his mother was difficult. Fromm describes her as depressive, narcissistic, and possessive. She was a housewife with no formal education, and focused entirely on her role as mother of her only child. "My mother was very much bound to her own family and really she liked me in as much I was a Krause, which was her family name, and everything which was good in me was typically Krause and everything bad was Fromm!" [1] To stress what belongs while denigrating "the other" indeed demonstrates a narcissistic pattern in the mother-son relationship. For a long time, the young Erich accepted this treatment without rebellion–at least so long as he pictured himself in the role of defender of his mother against his father.

For the possessed child, such a relationship always has two sides: on one hand he may feel idealized, held in high regard, admired and pampered; on the other, he feels in bondage to his mother–at the mercy of her whims; responsible for her but also under her control.

Erich Fromm and his mother

His mother acted out her dreams in the photographer's studio. Here, the young Fromm is cast as the daughter she never had.

A visit to the photographer was a popular custom around the turn of the century. The ritual seemed to have had a special attraction for Erich Fromm's mother. Here she could have the child photographed from all sides and in all sorts of costumes and poses. Here, she would have herself depicted in the glow of motherhood. She might fantasize that her son was a daughter, a sailor, a Bavarian shepherd boy.

Fromm's relationship with his mother can hardly be illustrated better: she clutches her son to her bossom as she gazes into the distance, while the weeping willow in the background seems to underscore the dreariness of such a relationship.

"My mother was not really interested in me as an individual either, she dreamed of my becoming a professional pianist. I was taught piano as most children of my class were and that ended when the war began in 1914; but my mother greatest hope was I would become a second Paderewski!"[1] (Ignacy Jan Paderewski was a celebrated Polish pianist of the period, also composer and politician, who became Prime Minister of Poland in 1919).

"My greatest wish was to play violin and for God knows what reason–I think because of Paderewski–I was sentenced to learn piano and so I had a great prejudice against piano."[1] Fromm acknowledged that he loved music despite his mother. He developed an aversion to playing the piano, however, and was happy when the lessons with his half-deaf piano teacher ended.

➤

One of the many postcards that Fromm's father mailed home every day when he was traveling. This one, dated the twenty-second of June, 1932, came from Hamburg. At the end of the card he writes: "So I will be home about 11p.m. Until a happy reunion–1000 greetings and kisses and best wishes, your faithful Neph."

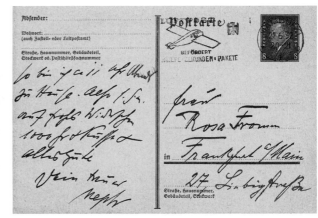

Naphtali Fromm's wine business determined the course of daily life at 27 Liebigstrasse in the west of Frankfurt. (Today, there is again a wine shop on the ground floor.) Of course, Fromm's father was often out and about on business. He generally sold his wines up to 200 kilometers (124 miles) around Frankfurt, and also had clients in Düsseldorf. Such business trips meant being away from his family, which the paterfamilias disliked. Even when he was out of the house for just one night, he would send a postcard.

In bourgeois-liberal circles at the beginning of the twentieth century, devotion to the family was considered an admirable goal. Even more so for the orthodox Fromms. Their religious practice and quest for an ideal family life turned the household into

something of a ghetto. The parents sought to maintain strict religious observance within the household. Although the community synagogue at Börneplatz under rabbi Nehemia Anton Nobel was a center of Orthodox Judaism, it was a good half an hour away to the east of the old city. The nearby synagogue in Freiherr vom Steinstrasse was, however, of a liberal persuasion. Rituals connected with food, prayer, the Sabbath, and religious holidays were thus centered on the family.

1913: the parents with
their only child in the wood
at Bad Homburg vor der
Höhe.

In 1989 Dr. Hans Hayn, still owner of the house at 27 Liebigstraße, remembers: "Always on Friday evening and on the Sabbath, there was a service in this house. One could hear Mr. Fromm with Jewish chants and prayers and addresses. They always maintained a very strict interpretation of the Sabbath. There were no walks; they would sit at home busy with their devotions." [6]

This kind of religious life contributed to the alienation of everything that might have been interesting outside the family–his father even saw the outside as a threat.

Life outside the house was entertained only within the protection of the family. There were mainly tours in the neighboring Taunus woods that might be combined with a visit to relatives in Bad Homburg vor der Höhe. And of course there were many Jewish acquaintances in the west of Frankfurt. From the second half of the nineteenth century, after a long struggle for emancipation, the Jews of Frankfurt were permitted to live outside the ghettos and many settled in the west end.

Family gathering in 1910 with Martha Stein, his mother's oldest sister from Berlin. From the right: Martha Stein, Rosa Fromm, Bernhard Stein, Charlotte Stein, and Erich Fromm.

Contacts with relatives on both sides of the family ranked especially high, the more so since Erich Fromm's mother blossomed in the extended family circle and became "full of life."

An aunt on his father's side, Zerline Fromm from Bad Homburg vor der Höhe, would look after Erich when his parents were traveling. His mother maintained close relations with her two older sisters. Sophie had married Dr. David Engländer in Berlin; she wrote the letter on page 49, before, in 1942 under the Nazi regime, the couple were transported to Theresienstadt concentration camp and murdered there.

Martha, the oldest sister of his mother, lived together with her husband, Bernhard Stein, at 14c Alexander-31strasse in Berlin. The Steins were especially close because their daughter, Charlotte, often spent her holidays–at least seven weeks a year–with Erich in Frankfurt.

26

Family gathering in 1916 in Bad Homburg vor der Höhe. From the left: Zerline Fromm, Erich's mother Rosa Fromm, her eldest sister Martha and her husband Bernhard Stein; Erich Fromm with his father Naphtali.

Charlotte Stein and Erich Fromm. Fromm's cousin, known as Lotte, was some two years older and was very friendly with Erich as she revealed as a ninety-year-old in a letter: "The relationship with Erich was like brother and sister."

A birthday letter from Erich to his mother, shortly after he had his appendix removed.

To my dear birthday girl:
Though I don't have an appendix any more, not even a little bit left,
I am so happy at your birthday, that I can be in our cosy home.
I brought you two small bowls for a present:
for hairpins I thought–so you can find them more readily.
And knife-rests for the table are quite useful too.
I don't have much, but every present comes from my heart.
May you see only bright sunshine in the circle of your family for 150 years!
The days should pass in bliss and happiness.
May G'd protect you wherever you stay, and may your good works serve you well, and may you celebrate your birthday in joy for many years–just as you do today.

Dem lieben Geburtstagskinder,
Hab ich auch keinen Blinddarm m
Auch keinen kleinen Rest,
So freue ich mich doch gar sehr
An Dein'm Geburtstagfest,
Dass ich nun sein kann zu Haus
In unsrer schönen heimschen
Paar kleine Schälchen hab ich mir
laubt,
Die zu machen zum Präsent:
„Für Haarnadeln hab ich geglaubt,
Damit man sie leichter fän

These close family bonds meant that–apart from school–Fromm had almost no contact with non-Jewish friends, children from the neighborhood or playmates. Among the many photographs that show the child and adolescent Erich Fromm there is not a single one that shows him together with children except for those photographs from school or family occasions. Everything focused on the child Erich within the nuclear and extended families.

Rosa Fromm loved to take her family on visits to resorts popular with the bourgeoisie. So young Erich became aquainted with Baden Baden, Montreux, Davos, St. Moritz, and probably also Locarno.

Auch Bänkchen für den Tisch
Sind gar so unnützlich nicht.
Viel ist's zwar nicht, was ich habe,
Doch von Herzen gern kommt jede Gabe.

Mögest im Kreise Deiner Familie
Der hellen Sonnenschein Du sehn
Und bis zu 150 Jahren
Die Tage in Wonne und Glück
Dir vergehen.

Möge G'tt Dich beschützen,
Wo Du auch immer wehst,
Und möge Dir nützen
Das Gute, das Du tust.
Und mögest Du feiern noch lange,
lange Zeit
Deinen Geburtstag in Frieden gehau sowie heut.

Photographs from holidays in Montreux, St. Moritz, Baden Baden.

29

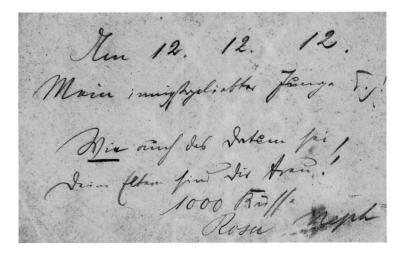

On the 12th of December, 1912, the twelve-year-old Erich received a postcard from his mother postmarked Frankfurt 12.12.12.

"My tenderly loved son Erich! Whatever the date may be, your parents are true to you!
1000 kisses
Rosa, Neph"

In the autobiographical notes to his book *Beyond the Chains of Illusion* (1962) Fromm devotes just one sentence to his moody, anxious father and his mother with her tendency to depression. He makes no mention of any impact that this psychological burden might have had on him, writing instead: "I started to get interested in those curious and mysterious origins of human reactions" [7] and recalls the suicide of a twenty-five-year-old painter, a friend of the family, whom the twelve-year-old found beautiful and fascinating. The young woman, however, was strongly attached to her unattractive, widowed father and committed suicide shortly after he died. In her will, she declared that she wanted to be buried with her father. Fromm notes that he dwelt on this incident more than on anything he had experienced to date.

Why should Fromm turn to this incident just after talking about his parents? Did this sucide–the result of a neurotic parental relationship–alarm him? The twelve-year-old begins by asking "How is this possible?"[8] and goes on to consider how destructive a neurotic fixation might become.

At twelve years of age, Erich still enjoyed sitting on his father's lap. He basked self-confidently in the admiration of his adored mother. Soon, however, he began to seek ways out of the childish relationship with his father and the narcissistic idealization and possessiveness of his mother.

31

2
"How Is This Possible?"
The Questioning Adolescent

This photograph of her son, printed as a postcard, was meant as a surprise for Erich's mother who was staying at her sister Martha's in Berlin. The card, franked the 3rd of December, 1912, in Frankfurt, was written by Oswald Sussmann, a Galician Jew who lived with the Fromms between 1912 and 1914. Fromm said he was the first person really to show interest in him.

Between 1912 and 1914, through outings and political discussions with Oswald Sussman, Erich found the beginnings of an escape from the stifling family circle. From about sixteen, he developed a lively interest in Rabbi Nobel and his circle of young people. Meanwhile, school and the search for teachers as role models of autonomy and independence became increasingly important.

Erich went to Wöhlerschule in Lessingstrasse, a school where he learned Latin, English, and French. In 1918, he finished his final school leaving examination here with distinction. The examination papers and his certificates were destroyed by fire during World War II together with the school. Fromm went to Wöhlerschule and not to the Philanthropin, a notable Jewish school, perhaps because the former was close to home and because a relatively high percentage–over 20 percent– of the pupils there were Jewish. Leo Löwenthal, a friend of Fromm's, went to Wöhlerschule; later Elias Canetti and Alfred Grosser attended this school as well.

Erich Fromm's memory of his school years was linked to World War I, the senseless inhumanity of which he did not at first understand.

The fourteen-year-old. Whether or not Erich was a good pupil remains unclear since school records were destroyed during World War II.

Pupils from Class III B on an excursion in May, 1913.

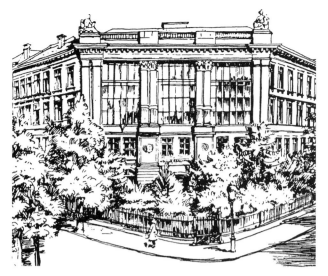

Wöhlerschule in Frankfurt's West End, which Erich Fromm attended from 1906 and where he took his final exam in 1918. It was destroyed during the war.

But this soon changed: "In our English class we had been given the assignment of learning by heart the British national anthem. This assignment was given us before the summer vacation, while there was still peace. When classes were resumed we boys, partly out of mischief and partly because we were infected by the 'hate England' mood, told the teacher that we refused to learn the national anthem of what was now our worst enemy. I still see him standing in front of the class, answering our protests with an ironical smile, and saying calmly: 'Don't kid yourselves; so far England has never lost a war!' Here was the voice of sanity and realism in the midst of insane hatred–and it was the voice of a respected and admired teacher! This one sentence and the calm, rational way in which it was said, was an enlightenment. It broke through the crazy pattern of hate and national self-glorification and made me wonder."[9]

In Wöhler-Gymnasium the fourteen-year-old found someone who dared to raise his voice against the common war cry, displaying autonomy and independence.

Erich Fromm (center front, looking to the right and wearing a headscarf) as member of a play group which gave a performance of *William Tell* on the 17th of November, 1914, in the Wöhlerschule.

The war years affected school life–teachers did not come back and pupils took wartime examinations. Nevertheless the tradition of school plays was maintained. Erich Fromm not only acted in Friedrich Schiller's *Wilhelm Tell* (*William Tell*), but took the role of the bride in Schiller's *Die Braut von Messina* (*The Bride of Messina*) in his final year.

The search for role models possessing a distinguished individuality and identity lasted throughout Fromm's life. The fact that he sought such people in religious traditions and movements was perhaps a result of his religious upbringing.

The adolescent changed his religious perspective when he discovered the messianic ideas of the Old Testament prophets. Such ideas became guiding principles not only in his religious, but also in his personal and social life.

Erich Fromm (second from right, for the first time wearing glasses) with classmates from the final school year in 1918 at Wöhler Realgymnasium in Frankfurt am Main.

Nehemia Anton Nobel,
rabbi of the synagogue at
Börneplatz in Frankfurt,
became Erich Fromm's
most important inter-
locutor between 1916 and
1921.

However much Fromm lived for his family, he tried to escape the restrictiveness of the household, dominated by religious ritual and fraught with religious angst. The first important means of escape was through Rabbi Dr. Nehemia Anton Nobel (1871-1922) of the Börneplatz synagogue in Frankfurt, who led the Orthodox Jewish community at that time. The second, from 1920, was through Dr. Salman Baruch Rabinkow from Heidelberg, a teacher of the Talmud in the Habad-Hasidic tradition, who witnessed Fromm's break with orthodoxy in 1926.

What is this "messianic idea" of the prophets according to Fromm's understanding?

Fromm had his own interpretation of the mission of the prophets. "Those who proclaim ideas and at the same time live them we may call prophets. The Old Testament prophets proclaimed the idea that man had

to find an answer to his existence, and this answer was the development of his reason, of his love. They taught that humility and justice were inseparably connected with love and reason. They lived what they preached. They did not seek power, not even the power of being a prophet; they avoided it. They were not impressed by might, and they spoke the truth even if this led to imprisonment, ostracism or death."[10]

This outline of the nature of prophetic mission (1967) demonstrates Fromm's preoccupation with the concept for decades.

Outside view of the synagogue at Börneplatz, where Rabbi Nobel taught and preached. (The photograph was taken after an extension was added in 1901.)

Inside the Börneplatz synagogue.

It contains just those elements, that the adolescent absorbed during services led by Rabbi Nobel and in discussions with him:

1. those who preach progressive ideas must practice them,
2. these ideas must take people's real questions and needs seriously and empower people to answer these questions and satisfy these needs,
3. power is not a means of realizing these ideas, rather love and moderation develop together with humility and justice.

The sixteen-year-old became acquainted, in an informal manner, with the messianic ideas of the prophets through discussions with Rabbi Nobel, who taught a mixture of Hasidic mysticism and the philosophy of the Enlightenment. Later Fromm discovered many such themes in the socialism of Karl Marx. Nobel, who was educated as a rabbi at the Hildesheimerschen Seminar in Berlin and "in his whole personality showed a strong and true Hasidic bent,"[11] had studied some time in Marburg with Hermann Cohen, of the New-Kantian school. Cohen moved later to Frankfurt and often came to Nobel's services in the synagogue at Börneplatz. He died in 1918.

Fromm mentions Nobel just once in his writing: "Nehemia Nobel was a mystic, deeply steeped in Jewish mysticism as well as in the thought of Western humanism."[12] In later conversations, however, he repeatedly referred to the charisma of this man.

When Rabbi Nobel preached in the Börneplatz synagogue, the philosopher Hermann Cohen was often in the congregation. Cohen, a New-Kantian, had great influence on Rabbi Nobel and on the young Fromm. (Painting by Max Liebermann, taken from Cohen's book *Religion der Vernunft*.)

Fromm introduced Ernst Simon to the Nobel circle. The teacher, who later moved to Jerusalem, called Erich Fromm his "most beloved friend"[16].

Their differing attitudes toward the state of Israel, however, occasionally strained their friendship.

Fromm and Nobel took long walks together on the edges of Frankfurt, even on the Sabbath, when, according to Jewish law, it was forbidden to walk more then a certain number of steps. Fromm also came for conversations to Nobel's apartment at 16 Börneplatz. In time, a small circle of mostly young people formed, a "kind of cult community," according to Leo Löwenthal, a school friend from Wöhlerschule, whom Fromm introduced to Nobel's circle.[13]

Ernst Simon, another important friend of Fromm's youth, also belonged to this circle. Löwenthal and Simon discovered a Judaism that was relevant to their lives through Fromm and the Nobel group. A few years later, also through Fromm's intervention, both underwent psychoanalysis on the couch of Frieda Reichmann in Heidelberg. Siegfried Kracauer also belonged to the group.

In spring 1919, the Jewish philosopher of religion, Franz Rosenzweig, heard Nobel preaching for the first

time and wrote in a letter to his mother: "He is an ingenious preacher. He speaks freely, with mastery, very simply; without a trace of unctuousness, unassuming even when he gets excited I have not heard anything like it before. A free mind, of the Cohen school, with a feel for words I am still ecstatic about it..."[14]

Georg Salzberger, a liberal rabbi in Frankfurt, promoted the idea of a Freies Jüdisches Lehrhaus (Free Jewish Teaching Institute), the first Jewish adult education center. Fromm played a decisive part in its foundation.

In the Nobel group, Fromm became familiar with Cohen's principal work, *Religion der Vernunft aus den Quellen des Judentums* (*The Religion of Reason from the Sources of Judaism*), a source of inspiration for his own interpretations of the bible. Through Nobel, Fromm also came into contact with Zionism and its youth organization, the Blau-Weiss Hikers' League, between 1919 and 1923. The Blau-Weiss, founded in 1913 was the first Zionist youth league in Germany. After World War I, the league made emigration to Palestine its main aim. Fromm played a leading role in forming the KJV (the Kartell Jüdischer Verbindungen—a group of Jewish organizations) in Frankfurt, whose aim was to turn its members into responsible Zionists.[15]

Ernst Simon circulated the oft-quoted "prayer of the little KJV. members": "*Mach mich wie den Erich Fromm, dass ich in den Himmel komm.*" ("Make me like Erich Fromm, so I will go to heaven!"[17] [The German word *fromm* means pious.])

Under the influence of Rabinkow, his new Talmudic teacher in Heidelberg, Fromm soon realized the extent to which Jewish nationalism was cultivated in the Zionist movement. This came into conflict with the humanistic interpretation of Judaism and Messianism he had absorbed from Cohen and Rabinkow. On his resignation in 1923 he argued that "In these years, I found Jewish nationalism no better than that of the *Hakenkreuzer* [swastika wearers]."[18]

Franz Rosenzweig ran the
Free Jewish Teaching
Institute in Frankfurt from
1920.

Martin Buber was also a
lecturer at the Free Jewish
Teaching Institute.

Fromm's renunciation of Zionism was definitive; he kept to this position throughout his life. Among other things, it meant he had little sympathy for the state of Israel and threw himself into the struggle for the rights of the Palestinians.

Rabbi Nobel's influence on Fromm's development, shows itself also in the leading role he played in the foundation of a Jewish educational center for adults, later to become Frankfurt's Freies Jüdisches Lehrhaus (Free Jewish Teaching Institute).

The idea came from Georg Salzberger, a young and liberal Frankfurt rabbi, who wanted to do something against the widespread ignorance of Jewish religion and history among the Jewish community. Salzberger remembers: "I consulted my young friend Erich Fromm who—since he came from an orthodox family—shared my interests. We founded together at the end of 1919 the *Vereinigung* (association) or as it was called later the Association for Jewish people's Education in Frankfurt am Main. The lecture session opened with a ceremony on the 22nd of February, 1920, in which Rabbi Nobel read a chapter from the Cabala." [19]

In the summer of 1920, Franz Rosenzweig became director of the society, which founded the Free Jewish Teaching Institute on the 17th of October of the same year.

On the agenda were the following points:
1. Calling a members' meeting.
2. Contract with Dr. Stall (codirector of the institute with Dr. Rosenzweig).
3. Powers of the advisory board.
4. Announcement of the program.
5. Prize-competition for a Purim game.

(The Purim game was usually a one act play of biblical content, which was performed at the Purim festival in springtime in Yiddish.)

Einladung zur Sitzung der Gesellschaft für jüd. Volksbildung E.V.

Mittwoch, den 26.9.23, abends 8½ Uhr

im Sitzungssaale der Königsteiner Synagoge.

Tagesordnung:

1.) Einberufung einer Mitgliederversammlung.

2.) Vertrag mit dem neben Herrn Dr Rosenzweig verantwortlich zeichnenden Leiter des Lehrhauses u. mit Herrn Dr. Stall.

3.) Befugnisse des Beirates.

4.) Kenntnisgabe des Programms.

5.) Preisausschreiben für ein Purimspiel.

i.A.:

Marie Schönfärber

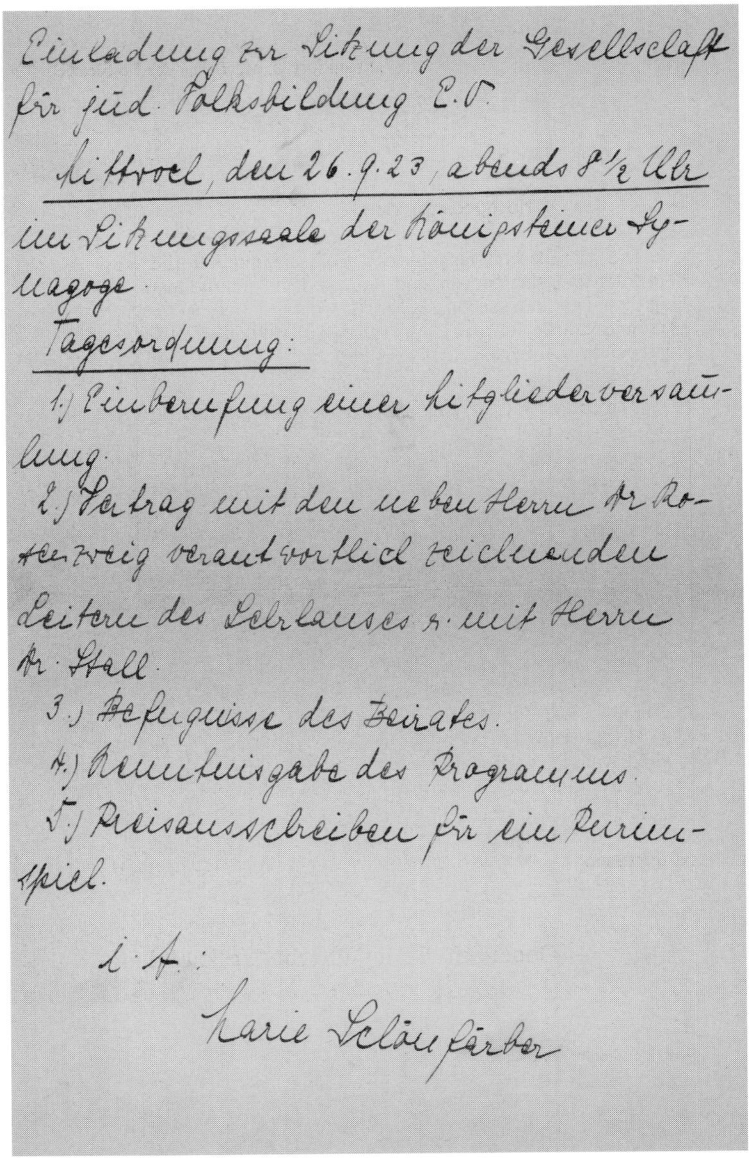

The Free Jewish Teaching Institute was supported by the Association for Jewish People's Education. This invitation by the association to a meeting on the 26th of September, 1923 in the assembly hall of the synagogue in Königstein demonstrates clearly its interests.

Nobel and his circle lectured here along with Franz Rosenstein, Martin Buber, Geshom Scholem, and Leo Baeck.

In 1923 Erich Fromm offered a seminar about the Jewish Karaite sect that he had studied for his doctorate. In the same year there was a summer school, in which Ernst Simon offered an introductory weekend course in Raschi (Salomo ben Isaak, 1040-1105). Erich Fromm led an advanced course about Raschi's commentary on Exodus and Gershom Scholem dealt with the book of Daniel and interpreted the Sohar (the main part of the Cabala).

In the winter of 1923-24 Salman Baruch Rabinkow, Erich Fromm's Talmud teacher from Heidelberg, also taught at the institute. Leo Baeck gave a guest lecture about God's love and the meaning of the religious service. In the seventh academic year, 1925-26, Leo Löwenthal lectured on Jewish history.

Frankfurt a. M., Datum des Poststempels.

Hochgeehrter Herr!

Die Gesellschaft für jüdische Volksbildung hat die Absicht, dem Interesse, das Sie ihr und dem von ihr unterhaltenen Freien Jüdischen Lehrhaus schon bisher bewiesen haben, nunmehr eine persönliche feste Form zu geben. Sie hat zu diesem Zweck die beiliegende Fördererkarte eingeführt, mit der für den Inhaber die Rechte eines

Förderers des Freien Jüdischen Lehrhauses

verbunden sind, nämlich

1. alle Rechte eines Mitgliedes der Gesellschaft für jüdische Volksbildung (Mitgliedsbeitrag mindestens 20 M.);

2. das Recht, in jedem Lehrgang des Lehrhauses zwei Vorlesungen oder Arbeitsgemeinschaften (also im Jahr sechs Veranstaltungen) unentgeltlich zu belegen;

3. das Recht, außerdem noch beliebig viele weitere Vorlesungen oder Arbeitsgemeinschaften zum halben Preise zu belegen.

Wir bitten Sie, die beiliegende Fördererkarte auf Ihren Namen oder den eines Ihrer Angehörigen auszufüllen und durch die beiliegende Zahlkarte den Jahresbetrag von zweihundert Mark (oder falls Sie die lebenslängliche Fördererschaft zu erwerben wünschen: dreitausend Mark) im Interesse einer geregelten Geschäftsführung uns möglichst umgehend zugehen zu lassen.

Falls Sie die Karte nicht zu behalten wünschen, bitten wir, sie unter Benutzung des vorgedruckten Briefumschlags uns wieder zurückzusenden.

Mit ausgezeichneter Hochachtung

Gesellschaft für jüdische Volksbildung.

Postscheckkonto No. 53009.

In one of the few books from Fromm's library in the Erich Fromm Archive in Tübingen from the period of his studies in Heidelberg was folded this invitation for a meeting of the Association for Jewish People's Education, the parent body of the Free Jewish Teaching Institute (left). The invitation was written on the back of a leaflet seeking sponsors for the institute.

The fruitful cooperation with Rabbi Nobel ended suddenly on the 24th of January, 1922, with his early death. On 21st of that month, the fifty-year-old had given a lecture on Goethe, and his relationship to religion and religions. Franz Rosenzweig recalls in his letters the extent of the loss. On the 25th of January, he wrote to Martin Buber: "You will already have seen in the paper the dreadful news which has struck us here. A fundamental part of life has been pulled from under my feet."

In the Frankfurt *Neuen Jüdischen Presse* (*New Jewish Press*) an obituary was published that February that has been ascribed to Fromm. In it he describes Nobel as a person who "lived what he said and only said that which he lived. He taught that love bound people together and we understood because he loved us. In humility he called on the prophets—we call in mourning for a leader!"

Here one begins to perceive how far Nobel had become a "charismatic rabbi, elevated to the state of a surrogate father."[20]

Fromm did his final examination in the spring of 1918 at the Wöhlerschule, then enrolled for two semesters' study of jurisprudence at Frankfurt University.

During the years he was connected with the Free Jewish Teaching Institute, however, Fromm visited Frankfurt merely as a guest. He had hoped to study the Talmud in Lithuania, but he did not want to burden his parents with the separation and anyway got a clear veto from them against his plan to travel so far away.

For the summer semester of 1919, Fromm went to study in Heidelberg—continuing the search for the personal fulfillment that was still alien to him as a result of his restricted upbringing. He did find some personal fulfilment in Heidelberg: with his Talmud teacher Rabinkow; with his doctoral supervisor, Weber; with his girlfriend (later his wife), Frieda Reichmann, and with the physician Georg Groddeck from Baden Baden.

Photographs sometimes shine a stronger light on family relationships than psychological analysis can.

Erich Fromm's parents.

On the gravestone—according to Jewish tradition—his forefathers and his most important achievements are mentioned:

"Here rests the scholar,
leader of our community
Mr. Naphtali Fromm s.A*
son of the great rabbi
the just, a pillar of the earth
Rabbi Seligmann Fromm s. A.
great-grandson of Gaon
Rabbi S. B. Bamberger s. A.
died on Sabbath 12th Teweth 5694.

He fought God's struggle for Judaism and
specifically in pious affairs for the Israelite religious
school and specifically for the Unterlindau
Synagogue of which he was the main pillar. Honey
and mildness were under his tongue, his wisdom
shone from his face. With beautiful words and with
the kindness of his heart he drew the hearts of
people to him."

Following two years in Davos, during which he recovered from tuberculosis, Fromm left, in autumn 1933, for a few weeks in the United States. Shortly afterwards, his father died. In early summer 1934, Fromm finally settled in the U.S.A..

After Fromm left Frankfurt, his father engaged himself ever more with the local Jewish community. As one of the two conservative delegates to the National Prussian Jewish Communities, he traveled widely. In 1919, he was a founding member of the Hermann Cohen Lodge in Frankfurt and was its president from 1924 to 1925. Fromm's father died just over a year after Hitler came to power on the 29th of December, 1933 in Frankfurt. His relatively early death at sixty-four meant an especially heavy loss for the Unterlindau synagogue. This is clear from the obituaries for "the factory owner Naphtali Fromm."

Rabbi Jakob Horovitz writes that no other institution had grown closer to him then the "house of God," the Unterlindau synagoge. "He was its cofounder and promoter and its most active board member. He served us selflessly for decades with his masterly command of our liturgy and Frankfurt's Minhag ritual, through his exemplary reading of the Megilla (book roll), and as lector at festival services even during the troubling months of heavy illness almost into the last weeks of his life."[21]

*seligen Andenkens: of blessed remembrance

46

Rosa Fromm, Erich Fromm's mother lived in New York from 1941.

Whenever Fromm was in New York he always visited his mother who lived there until 1959.

For a while, Fromm's mother stayed on in Frankfurt, leaving the flat at 27 Liebigstraße and moving five streets on into number 8, Körnerwiese. In May, 1936 Fromm cashed in his deposit book in Frankfurt and had the savings transferred to his mother. Additionally he sent money in the summer of 1936 so she could visit him in New York. From September until November 1936 his mother was with him in New York, but returned to Frankfurt according to plan. From June 1937 he transferred as much money to her as was allowed.

German troops marched into Austria on the 12th of March, 1938, and, after the Munich agreement in September, 1938, Czechoslovakia was forced to hand over to the Reich those parts of Bohemia and Moravia—the Sudetenland—where many Germans lived. Fromm was convinced that Hitler would soon start a war and put pressure on his mother to emigrate. But she did not want to leave Germany.

In the autumn of 1938, Fromm sent an affidavit stating that he would support her if she left Germany and took refuge in another country. It was only after *Kristallnacht* in November 1938 that his mother wrote him that she now definitely wanted to leave.

Fromm wrote to Max Horkheimer on the 1st of December, 1938, in order to borrow a part of the money he needed as a surety for his mother from the Institute for Social Research:

"The situation is now, that she can come to the U.S.A. in about one and a half years (I sent her, in any case, an affidavit two months ago) but in the meantime she can stay in England or Switzerland (?) if she can deposit about $U.S. 1000. The money would be secure, because it is not to be used. I now want to ask you, if the cash box of the institute could lend me U.S.$ 500 (against interest—I am suggesting this, because it might make things perhaps 'formally' easier. Financially it does not play a big role). I asked Frau H[orney] for the other $500. My wife [Frieda Fromm-Reichmann] just had to spend $5000 on her siblings and so can't [help] at the moment. In case it's not possible, please send me a cable, so I do not raise false hopes in my mother."

Aunt Sophie and uncle David Engländer from Berlin. They wrote this letter to relatives before they were murdered in the concentration camp at Theresienstadt.

Horkheimer immediately cabled that the institute had no more money for this purpose. His mother managed, however, to find refuge in England for two years until Fromm was finally able to bring her to New York in 1941. There she lived her own life in contact with other emigrants. At the age of eighty-three she died of cancer in New York on the 26th of February, 1959 and was buried in Beth-El cemetery in New Jersey.

Other relatives on his father's and mother's side also managed to escape the concentration camps through early emigration (mostly to South America). But those who stayed were to perish in Hitler's death factories as this last letter from Fromm's maternal aunt, Sophie Engländer, bears witness.

Berlin, 29th August, 1942

To all my most beloved children and grand children!

For your birthday, dear William, we were at the parents' house and drank coffee to your health. They traveled to Theresienstadt near Prague a few days later. We will probably travel there soon too, although we do not yet know the exact date. We are glad that we will meet each other there again. Also, Father Br.'s friend, Dr. Alexander, as well as aunt Flore and countless friends and acquaintances. Aunt Hulda will leave her flat the day after tomorrow. It's apparently good there for us old people, especially the climate and the scenery. Unfortunately Uncle Martin and Aunt Johanna are not there. We have not had any news from them for a few weeks and that worries me, because Uncle Martin was still weak after his gallbladder illness...
I will miss seeing any children in Th[eresienstadt].. Keep healthy and don't worry about us. I repeat this always in every letter, because I do not know which one will be received: we have had many good things and much beauty in our life, good children and grand children who were our joy...
Despite the dreadful things which are happening, there is still much that is beautiful in the world. Father and I do not give up hope for a reunion. Please greet all our loved ones, Aunt Martha, the Hirschfelds, the Steins, Aunt Rosinchen [Erich Fromm's mother], Erich, Altmanns, Meta, Ita and husband, Greti, Aunt Irma and family. How nice it was that we were so lucky to know so many good and dear people in our life...

Your grandma and grandpa.

3
Apprenticeship of the Soul: From Talmudic Studies to Psychoanalysis

After two semesters studying law in Frankfurt, Fromm enrolled in a course in jurisprudence at Ruprecht-Karls University in Heidelberg on the 6th of May, 1919.

Records show that he registered for a lecture course and seminars on the German civil code but also that he was interested mainly in history. Fromm signed up for lectures on "German History of the Middle Ages" given by Hermann Oncken and "A History of Psychology" offered by Karl Jaspers. He also attended lectures by Hans Driesch (who was later to become a parapsychologist) on "the History of Philosophy."

Sommer ~~Winter~~-Semester 192 *2*   Einzugsliste O.-z2375

Zahlung

durch stud. *phil*   (Vor- und Familienname) *Erich Fromm*

aus (Geburtsort) *Frankfurt M.*   (Staatsangehörigkeit) *Preußen*

Heimatadresse *Frankfurt H. Liebigstr. 27.*

a) Vorlesungen und Uebungen	b) Namen der Lehrer	Honorar ℳ	Prakt.-Beitrag ℳ	Bemerkungen
Allgem. Volkswirtschaftslehre	Prof. Weber	50	✓	
Volksw. Übungen	Prof. Gothein	20	✓	
Volksw. Übungen	Prof. Weber	20	✓	
Soziologische Übungen	Prof. Weber	fr.	✓	
Wirtschafts- u. Kulturgesch. Mittelalt.	Prof. Gothein	30	✓	
Deutsches Reichs- u. Landesstaatsrecht	Prof. Thoma	50	✓	
Deutsches Verwaltungsrecht	Prof. Ausschütt	50	✓	
Allgem. Staatslehre u. Politik	Prof. Thoma	40	✓	
Entstehung d. neuen Testament	Prof. Dibelius	10	✓	
Schleiermacher a. Theologe u. a. Religionsphilosoph	Prof. Wobbermin	10	✓	

Honorare 210
Praktikantenbeiträge . . . . .
Studiengebühr 80
Seminargebühr 40
Institutsgebühr . . . . .
Bibliothekgebühr 10
Beitrag zur akadem. Lesehalle 5
Akad. Krankenverein 30
Studentenausschuß 14
Unfallversicherung 4
Beitrag für „mensa academica" 6
Turn- und Sportamt 7

During the summer semester of 1922, Fromm enrolled among others for the following lectures and seminars: "Political Economy", "Economic and political studies" (with Alfred Weber), "Economic and Cultural History of the Middle Ages" (with Gothein), "German National and State Law", "Universal Constitutional Law and Politics" (with Thoma), and "Development of the New Testament" (with Dibelius).

Apart from history, Fromm displayed an interest in courses on economics. In the winter of 1919-20, he attended: "Money and Credit" and "the Stock Exchange and Trade Law." In this semester, he first enrolled for lectures on politics and sociology: "Social Politics and Social Movements," "Problems of Socialization." and "Theory of Marxism."

To begin with, Fromm lived in the suburbs of Heidelberg (largely destroyed in World War II), at 61 Bergheimer-straße and later found lodging with the Marx family on the second floor of 64 Plöck–a street within the old city of Heidelberg. During the 'twenties, Karl Jaspers lived in the house next door. It was just a stone's throw from the university library.

In the winter semester of 1920-21, Fromm finally switched faculties and studied in the department of National Economy (sociology had not yet achieved departmental status in Heidelberg).

As his most important university teacher Fromm would always mention Alfred Weber (1869-1958) the brother of Max Weber who died in 1920.

"I had only one non-Jewish teacher whom I really admired and who deeply influenced me and that was Alfred Weber, the brother of Max, also a sociologist but in contrast to Max, a humanist not a nationalist, and a man of out-standing courage and integrity. I attended his lectures and seminars for many years and often things he said went above my head (I must add that he did talk sometimes in a somewhat bizarre and con-fusing language) but he was the only one of my university teachers whom I considered a

Fromm's student digs were at 64 Plöck (with flag), a street in the old city of Heidelberg.

Alfred Weber, Fromm's supervisor. In a letter to Weber, on 23rd December, 1955, his former student wrote: ".. studies with you were one of the most fertile experiences [of] my life; not only in what I learned but also through your personality as a model."

real teacher and master. My relationship to him, however, remained very distant, because I was shy. It became more distant when, after my promotion, he mentioned that I might be interested in an academic career.

I felt so deeply that this was not for me and that such a career would restrain me, that I avoided seeing him alone, as far as I could, for the next two years."[22]

There was another teacher and master in Heidel-berg: Salman Baruch Rabinkow (1879-1941). Erich Fromm had a very close relationship with this private scholar who came from Russia.

Rabinkow lived a strictly orthodox and ascetic life in a furnished room at 14 Rahmengasse in Heidelberg. He had extensive knowledge of the history of Jewish ideas and sympathized with the thinking of the New Kantian Hermann Cohen, with Zionist activists and with socialist revolutionaries.

Salman Rabinkow, a Hasidic scholar of the Talmud, was Fromm's most important teacher in Heidelberg between 1920 and 1925.

ספר
לקוטי אמרים
חלק ראשון
הנקרא בשם
ספר של בינונים
מלוקט מפי ספרים ומפי סופרים קדושים עליון נ"ע מיוסד על
פסוק כי קרוב אליך הדבר מאוד בפיך ובלבבך לעשותו · לבאר
היטב איך הוא קרוב מאד בדרך ארוכה וקצרה בעזה"י ·

ונתוסף בו אגרת התשובה מאדמו"ר נ"ע בדרך ארוכה וקצרה
בכלל כל ענייני התשובה גם אגרת הקודש אשר כתב בכתב
ידו הקדושה ולשונו הטהור ·

כי אלה חוברו יחדיו תמים מלמעלה עיר וקדיש משמיא נחית

הוא ניהו כ"ק אדמו"ר הגדול הגאון האלקי אור עולם
מופת הדור נזר ישראל ותפארתו קדוש ה' מכובד
מרנא ורבנא שניאור זלמן נכג"מ ·

מחדש הובא הדתוצאה החדשה והמתקנת בזיו נמרץ כמבואר סע"ד.

ווילנא
בדפוס האלמנה והאחים ראם
שנת בקדוש ישראל יגילו לפ"ק

"I was Rabinkow's student for about five or six years and, if I remember correctly, I visited him at that time almost daily. The bulk of the time was occupied with studying Talmud, the rest with studying certain philosophical writings of Maimonides, the Schneur Salman's *Tanya*, Weiss's Jewish History, and a discussion of sociological problems. He took great interest and was very helpful in my doctoral dissertation. Rabinkow influenced my life more than any other man, perhaps, and although in different forms and concepts, his ideas have remained alive in me.

He was a man with whom one could never, even at the first meeting, feel oneself a stranger. It was as if one were continuing a conversation or relationship which had always existed. And that was necessarily so, because of his attitude. There was no polite small talk, no careful probing, no questioning appraisal of his visitor, but an immediate openness, concern, participation. I was never shy in front of Rabinkow. I do not remember a single instance in which I felt afraid of his judgment, of what he might say of this or of that, that he might 'judge' me; nor did he try to influence me, to tell me what to do, to admonish me. All his influence was his being, his example, although he was the last man to want to present an example. He was just himself."[23]

Many who knew Fromm describe Fromm himself in similar terms.

Confirmation by Prof. Curtius that Erich Fromm has passed the oral examination for his doctorate and qualifies for his certificate.

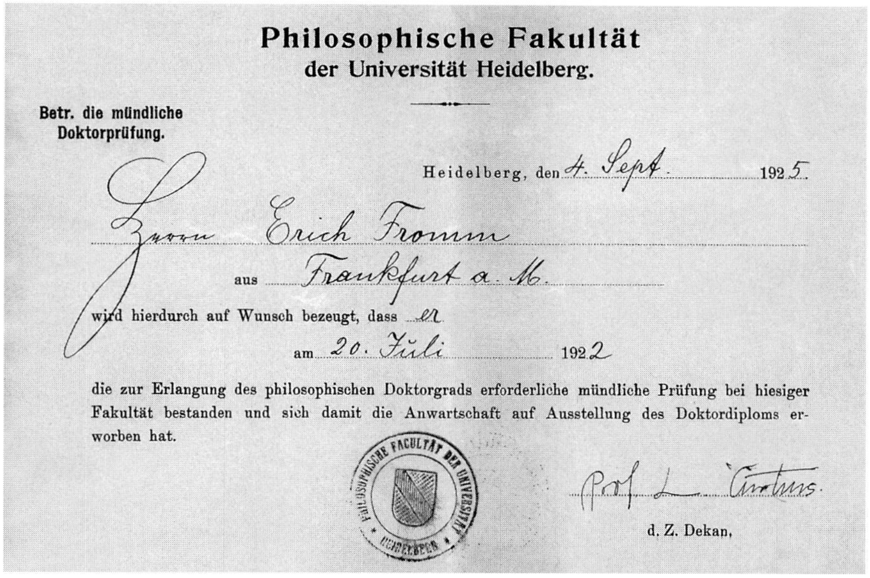

Philosophische Fakultät
der Universität Heidelberg.

Betr. die mündliche Doktorprüfung.

Heidelberg, den 4. Sept. 1925.

Herrn Erich Fromm

aus Frankfurt a. M.

wird hierdurch auf Wunsch bezeugt, dass er

am 20. Juli 1922

die zur Erlangung des philosophischen Doktorgrads erforderliche mündliche Prüfung bei hiesiger Fakultät bestanden und sich damit die Anwartschaft auf Ausstellung des Doktordiploms erworben hat.

PHILOSOPHISCHE FACULTÄT DER UNIVERSITÄT HEIDELBERG

Prof. L. Curtius.
d. Z. Dekan.

Fromm's affinity for Hasidism was more a result of the influence of Rabinkow, his Talmud teacher from Heidelberg, than that of Rabbi Nobel or Martin Buber. With Rabinkow, he studied the *Likutej Amarim* (collected sayings) of Schneur Zalman of Liadi in Lithuania, who founded Habad-Hasidism in the eighteenth century. The illustration shows the title page of the first edition of the *Likutej Amarim*. This book accompanied Fromm throughout his life and is now in the Fromm archive at Tübingen in Germany.

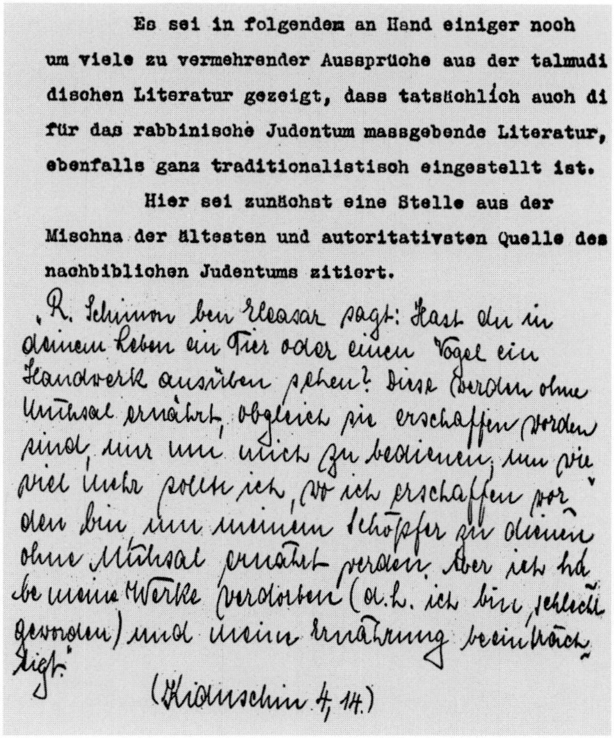

Es sei in folgendem an Hand einiger noch um viele zu vermehrender Aussprüche aus der talmudi dischen Literatur gezeigt, dass tatsächlich auch di für das rabbinische Judentum massgebende Literatur, ebenfalls ganz traditionalistisch eingestellt ist.

Hier sei zunächst eine Stelle aus der Mischna der ältesten und autoritativsten Quelle des nachbiblischen Judentums zitiert.

„R. Schimon ben Eleasar sagt: Hast du in deinem Leben ein Tier oder einen Vogel ein Handwerk ausüben sehen? Diese werden ohne Mühsal ernährt, obgleich sie erschaffen worden sind, nur um mich zu bedienen, um wie viel mehr sollte ich, der ich erschaffen worden bin, um meinem Schöpfer zu dienen ohne Mühsal ernährt werden. Aber ich habe meine Werke verdorben (d.h. ich bin schlecht geworden) und meine Ernährung beeinträchtigt."

(Kidduschin 4, 14)

Part of a manuscript of Fromm's dissertation, which he finished in 1922, with handwritten additions.

Fromm was twenty-two when he presented his dissertation for examination by Alfred Weber. In it, he examines the function of Jewish law in maintaining social cohesion in three Diaspora communities.

The Jewish Diaspora is remarkable for continuing to exist as a coherent group, bound together by blood and destiny, despite the loss of state, territory, and a common secular language and denied the opportunity to build places of worship.

Fromm later talked of the Jewish "social body" as being saturated in Jewish law. It formed a kind of "social cement." This social cohesion is made possible by that "law-abiding" ethos with which Jews of the Diaspora distinguish themselves from their "host-peoples." This is how they were able to "live among other peoples, within and outside their own world."[24]

Erich Fromm (first row, seated, third from left) with fellow students from the Association of Zionist Students in the summer of 1919. The photograph was taken in front of the Friedrichsbau in Heidelberg.

In his dissertation, Fromm's approach was primarily sociopsychological, although he did not yet have the instruments of psychoanalysis to explain how Jewish communities were unconsciously bound together through the daily practice of their belief system. What he wrote here about the function of Jewish Law (in the sense of an applied religious moral code) he later applied to the "libido structure or organization of social entities." After he abandoned the libido theory, he described the working of the social character in a similar way. It guarantees continuity and inner coherence among various manifestations of social groups. It is the "cement" that holds them together, because the common belief system encourages common ways of doing things, which in turn promote group solidarity in thinking, feeling, and acting.

In his dissertation, Fromm already recognizes that, if a social group organizes its way of life–its production, its socialization and types of relationships, its cultural, political, ethical and religious activities–in a way that promotes and stabilizes an outdated morality (even under changed circumstances), then the cohesion of that group is guaranteed. It was only with the help of Freud's psychoanalysis that Fromm understood that these manifestations of morality are to be understood as psychological structures, which constitute a dynamic, autonomous force. But the cross-fertilization of morality and life-style was already known in 1922.

Ruprecht-Karls-Universität-Heidelberg

Rektorat des Professors Dr. Karl Hampe.

Die Philosophische Fakultät hat dem

Herrn Erich Fromm

geboren 1900 zu Frankfurt a. M.

Titel und Würde eines Doktors der Philosophie verliehen. Die vorgelegte wissenschaftliche Abhandlung ‚Das jüdische Gesetz. Ein Beitrag zur Soziologie des Diasporajudentums' ist genehmigt und die mündliche Prüfung am 20. Juli 1922 abgelegt worden. Die Fakultät hat das Gesamtergebnis beider Leistungen als sehr gut (2. Grad) anerkannt. Fachvertreter war Professor Dr. Alfred Weber. ☙ Gegenwärtige Urkunde ist zu Heidelberg im 540. Jahr seit Gründung der Universität am 4. September 1925 vollzogen worden.

Siegel der Philosophischen Fakultät   Dekan der Philosophischen Fakultät

The Ph.D. certificate from
1925.

With this certificate, Heidelberg University awarded Erich Fromm the title and honor of Doctor of Philosophy. "The scientific discourse which was presented: 'Jewish Law, A Contribution to the Sociology of Diaspora-Judaism,' has been approved and the oral examination took place on the 20th of July, 1922. The faculty has approved the overall mark of both pieces of work as very good (second grade). The faculty specialist representative was Prof. Dr. Alfred Weber. This certificate is issued in Heidelberg in the 540th year of the university on 4th September, 1925."

Now Fromm's life took a decisive turn away from Orthodox Judaism and toward psychoanalysis. His friend, Frieda Reichmann (1889-1957), whom he later married, was instrumental in this development. Reichmann was eleven years older than Fromm, a psychiatrist, who had grown up and studied medicine in Königsberg. Between 1918 and 1920, she lived in Frankfurt, employed as an assistant by the psychiatrist Kurt Goldstein (1878-1965).

In 1920 she went to Dresden, taking up a job at the Weißer Hirsch sanatorium. There she became an assistant physician with Johannes Heinrich Schultz, who had become known for his autogenous training techniques of relaxation.

The Therapeuticum for psychoanalysis at 15 Mönchhofstrasse in Heidelberg. It was directed by Frieda Reichmann and Erich Fromm between 1924 and 1928.

The young Frieda Reichmann. In Dresden, Frieda Reichmann discovered Freud's writings and Freud's explanations about transference between patient and doctor.

Apart from her work in Dresden, she began a psycho-analytical education in Munich with Wilhelm Wittenberg which she subsequently continued with Hanns Sachs in Berlin.

Fromm already knew Frieda Reichmann from her period in Frankfurt. Another connection was through Golde Ginsburg, to whom Fromm had been briefly engaged (until his friend Leo Löwenthal fell in love with and married her). Ginsburg also hailed from Königsberg and was an old friend of Frieda Reichmann. After the engagement to Ginsburg was broken off, Fromm became friends with Reichmann, like him at that time a strictly observant Jew. He visited her now and then in Dresden. And so he discovered Freudian psychoanalysis.

Fascinated by Freud's discoveries, both decided to open a "therapeuticum" for Jewish patients in which Freudian psychoanalysis was to be applied. The idea was to help people through making them aware of their repressions. During an autobiographical interview, Frieda Fromm-Reichmann remembers: "We thought if it's right that people get well by having that which is repressed come into awareness, if that's right for the individual then it should also be right for the Jewish people as a group." [25]

During the period of hyperinflation in Germany in 1923, Fromm and Reichmann begged and borrowed the money for buying and furnishing a house at 15 Mönchhofstrasse in Heidelberg.

Frieda Reichmann on her Therapeuticum in Heidelberg:

"My God, how I worked in those [days] because you see the money had to be given back What did I get? Twenty-five thousand that was all. Fifteen I had to give back and ten I got as gifts.

"The way we built that thing up [was:] I would sit in a room with a patient and analyze and look around and I'd see oh we need curtains for this room. As the next fee came in from somebody, I'd go and buy those curtains. "And so we got the thing gradually going. Then we analyzed people [as compensation] for letting them work. I analyzed the housekeeper, I analyzed the cook.

"You may imagine what happened if they were in a phase of resistance! It was a wild affair, and I may add we later decided to cut it out. Erich and I had an affair. We weren't married and nobody was supposed to know about that and actually nobody did know." [25]

"The rhythm of Jewish daily life was an integral element in the spiritual atmosphere of this purely Jewish community. At meals, grace was said and there were homilies from traditional Jewish literature; the Sabbath and feast days were celebrated. All this led to the institute's being nicknamed the 'Thorapeuticum'."[26]

In contrast to the regulated Jewish life of the house community, with its kosher food, Sabbath-rituals and common prayer times, the therapeutic concept was quite unregulated; everybody landed on Frieda's couch and was analyzed: Erich himself, his friends Ernst Simon and Leo Löwenthal and his wife Golde, the Talmud-teacher Rabinkow—even his household staff including the cook. The richer Jewish clients often had little interest in revealing their repressions, but came from Frankfurt for the kosher food at weekends. The love-affair which had grown out of the therapeutic relationship between Erich and Frieda led to their marriage on the 16th of June, 1926, which happened to be the wedding anniversary of Erich Fromm's parents! Because of Frieda's tonsilitis, however, it almost fell through. But Frieda remembers: "I got what I wanted: a very intelligent, very warm, very well-educated man who knew lots of things in another field from mine."[25] Even before their marriage, Erich Fromm had moved to Munich for further education. He accepted financial support for this from Frieda Fromm-Reichmann, since he believed his father would not be able to handle his son's being psychoanalyzed. Like Reichmann before him, he now attended psychiatric lectures given by Kraepelin and continued his psychoanalysis with Wilhelm Wittenberg.

Psychoanalysis affected both of their attitudes toward religion. Dissatisfied with the lack of interest of the Jewish patients in the psychoanalytical concept of the Therapeuticum, Fromm-Reichmann remembers: "We decided we couldn't [do] it any longer because our conscience and hearts were no longer in it. So at Passover, Erich and I went into [the] park in Heidelberg and ate leavened bread. We couldn't do it at home because there were these people, who after all relied on us."[25]

The "fall from grace"—the renunciation of strictly orthodox religious observance—found its literary expression from both of them in the psychoanalytical magazine *Imago*. In 1927, Fromm-Reichmann published an article on Jewish food rituals and Fromm an article about the Sabbath.[27] This was his first article on psychoanalysis. Convinced of Freud's libido theory, Fromm interpreted the Sabbath ritual in 1927 in a way that left very little room for a religious Sabbath ritual at the Therapeuticum in Heidelberg: "The Sabbath was originally regarded as the remembrance of the killing of the father and the winning of the mother, the work ban is at the same time repentance for the original sin and its repetition through regression at the pregenital level."[28]

At the same time his interpretation reflects his own psychological change, which went on through the renunciation of the religion of his fathers and the turning to a motherly woman and to psychoanalysis. It still took one more year before they both decided to abandon the Therapeuticum altogether.

In 1928, Fromm went to finish his psychoanalytical training in Berlin, with Hanns Sachs at the Karl Abraham Institute. Fromm-Reichmann set up a private practice at the same time at 15 Mönchshofstrasse.

Erich Fromm knew Freud's psychoanalysis through his friend, and later wife, Frieda Reichmann.

The Marienhöhe Sanatorium in Baden Baden (now the Tanneneck Hotel) at 14, Werderstrasse. Here Frieda Fromm-Reichmann, Erich Fromm, Sándor Ferenczi, and Karen Horney met with Georg Groddeck.

An account of Erich Fromm's Heidelberg period would be incomplete without a mention of Georg Groddeck (1866-1934), who had an enormous influence on him. Groddek was director of the Marienhöhe Sanatorium close to the spa rooms in Baden Baden and a specialist in therapeutic massage. Initially, he was a friend of Fromm-Reichmann's.

She saw him often and they corresponded regularly, enabling Erich Fromm to make the acquaintance of this extraordinary personality.

"When I think of all analysts in Germany I knew, he was, in my opinion, the only one with truth, originality, courage and extraordinary kindness. He penetrated the unconscious of his patient, and yet he never hurt. Even if I was never his student in any technical sense, his teaching influenced me more than that of other teachers I had. He was a man of such stature, that the majority of the psychoanalysts in Germany were not capable of appreciating him, and he was too proud a man to make himself pleasant and popular."[29]

On their regular visits to Baden Baden, the Fromms also met Karen Horney and Sándor Ferenczi, who also regularly visited Baden Baden from Budapest. Fromm's theoretical views and therapeutic practice were influenced greatly during conversations in Baden Baden.

Fromm originated his critique of the mechanistic and patriarchal tendency of Freud's theories of libido, culture, and history, the universality of the Oedipus complex, the theory of penis envy, etc. in Baden Baden. Later the critique was developed by all involved.

The *Soul Searcher*, a psychoanalytical novel by Georg Groddeck, with a cover illustration showing a silhouette.

Even more important to Fromm was the way Groddeck understood illness. "Many illnesses are the product of people's lifestyles. If one wants to heal them, one has to change a patient's way of life; only in very few cases can the illness itself be tackled through so-called specifica," Groddeck wrote in his dissertation as early as 1889.[30]

Similarly, Groddeck's manner of dealing with his patients was unusual at that time. Fromm experienced Groddeck's direct humanity when he himself was a patient.

In July 1931 he fell ill with tuberculosis and had to live a long time apart from Frieda in Switzerland. Groddeck understood Fromm's illness as an expression of his wish to separate from his wife, at the same time showing his difficulty in coming to terms with this idea. He told this plainly and forcefully to Fromm, but also with empathy and understanding.

The process of deciding to separate from his wife took a long time and only when his inner separation was completed could he leave Davos and accept Karen Horney's invitation to be a guest lecturer at the Psychoanalytical Institute of Franz Alexander in Chicago.

In the obituary he wrote for Groddeck, Fromm described how impressed he had been by Groddeck's typical "motherly kindness" a trait shared by Ferenczi.

"[Neither was an] intellectual. In contrast to most other analysts who are mostly concerned with the manipulation of theories, Groddeck and Ferenczi were human beings who empathized with the person they wanted to understand and, I would say, who felt in themselves what the so-called patient was telling them; they were persons of great humanity and for them the patient was not an object but a partner. It is very characteristic, for example, [of] Ferenczi, that when a patient left a session [he] would [say] thank you. This was not a matter just of courtesy (even in that respect it would be very rare) but an expression of his feeling, of sharing with the patient."[1]

After separation from Erich, Frieda Fromm-Reichmann kept in touch with Groddeck. Printed on the next page is an excerpt from a letter she wrote on 29th August, 1933, from Montana-Crans in Switzerland to Groddeck. The uneasy beginning reflects her experience that, at the time when Hitler came to power, most of her non-Jewish friends turned away from her and she had to give up her practice in Heidelberg.

"I don't know how my life will unfold in the future; but somewhere I'll find a field of activity and the inner calmness out of which longing can become productive. My husband is better now and I believe that now the psychological requirements for his physical recovery have ripened in him and I am very happy about that."—And how are you, dear Dr. Groddeck?"

Georg Groddeck
(caricature by a patient from 1926)

Wartend

20.7.26

Groddeck was not very well at all. He had seriously underestimated the political situation in Hitler's Germany. Frieda Fromm-Reichmann had to move her practice to Strasbourg. She managed to get Groddeck to Switzerland for a lecture where he broke down and was taken to Medard Boss in the Burghölzli clinic. Shortly afterwards she visited him again in Zurich on her way to Palestine. Groddeck died in Zurich in the summer of 1934.

Alfred Weber, Salman Baruch Rabinkow, Frieda Fromm-Reichmann, Georg Groddeck—all were Fromm's teachers during his educational years in Heidelberg.

It was not merely the intellectual abilities of these teachers that helped shape Fromm; each had a personal aura that impressed him greatly.

Fromm was still learning. His first experiences of the unconscious and repression were on the couch in 15 Mönchshofstrasse.

Karen Horney, who was close to Fromm in the 'thirties, also belonged to Georg Groddeck's circle (drawing by Arthur Libov).

Sándor Ferenczi, too, was often a guest at Georg Groddeck's sanatorium in Baden Baden.

Excerpt from a letter written by Frieda Fromm-Reichmann to Georg Groddeck on the 29th of August, 1933

These were followed by psychoanalysis by Wilhelm Wittenberg in Munich. Through his wife, Fromm also had therapeutic contact with Karl Landauer in Frankfurt. Eventually, his wish to be trained in psychoanalysis led Fromm to Berlin, where he was analyzed by Hanns Sachs. In 1930, he completed his training and opened his own practice at 1 Bayrischer Platz in Berlin.

Though Fromm never met Freud and never tired of criticizing his instinct theory there is no doubt that he admired Freud throughout his life for having discovered how to access the unconscious.

"Freud opened a new world for me, the world of the unconscious. He taught me–and many millions–that we are conscious of only a small part of ourselves. He distinguished two kinds of the unconscious: the so-called preconscious–something which could be conscious, but is not at the moment (because one would go insane if one always thought about everything which goes on in one's brain at the same time). Then there is the unconscious—the sense of the repressed which is prevented by some force within me from becoming conscious. Shame, vanity, envy–all sorts of feelings can lead to repression and often do."[2]

Almost everybody who became acquainted with psychoanalysis in those days felt the urge to understand reality anew through what swirled into consciousness on the couch: repressions, fantasies, hopes, conflicts, and needs. Almost everybody published insights into this new way of understanding. Psychoanalysis was still far from considering itself as mainly a method for treating neurotic illnesses.

At that time, psychoanalysis was not the preserve of doctors and clinical psychologists. This doubtless enriched it and drew many people to learn more about it. The early psychologists came, accordingly, from a variety of professions.

Equally, psychoanalytical insights were applied to a wide range of fields. With the joy of discovery, artists, writers, doctors, criminologists, educators, developmental psychologists, and anthropologists reexamined their subjects.

At the same time, there was a reinterpretation of social and historical processes, the comparative studies of civilization, law, and politics. New light was shed on such pressing questions as war fever or women's rights.

Sigmund Freud on a visit to Berlin in 1928, shown here together with his daughter, Anna.

Accordingly, for the most part, Fromm sought an exchange of views with psychoanalysts of a socialist or Marxist tendency, such as Siegfried Bernfeld, Ernst Simmel, and Wilhelm Reich. He shared Karen Horney's doubts about the Oedipus complex and the patriarchal version of the instinct theory that had been nurtured at Groddeck's house. The urge to translate their own psychoanalytical experiences into action, to apply them to social and cultural phenomena, was strong and led to the impressive creativity of psychoanalysis during those years.

Fromm, a sociologist with some education in religious studies, jurisprudence and psychiatry had a specific interest in the insights of psychoanalysis. The theme of his dissertation on the function of Jewish law in binding together Jews of the Diaspora was treated from a sociopsychological perspective.

Ever since Fromm became acquainted with psychoanalysis, the question of the social unconscious—the unconscious of societies—was on his mind: those unconscious motivations that bind people together in classes, nations, religious, intellectual or professional communities; the unconscious drives or attitudes that bring them to think, feel, and behave in the same manner.

During his training in psychoanalysis, the development of Fromm's specific interests, which led to his insights in this field, can be seen in his contemporary lectures and publications. He held his first lecture in Berlin on the 18th June, 1927 on "The Healing of a Case of Lung Tuberculosis during Psychoanalytical Treatment." (!)

Nine months later, on the 18th March, 1928, he gave a lecture in Berlin on "The Psycho-analysis of the petty bourgeois."

The problem area of "Psychoanalysis and Sociology" was the theme of the Southwest German Psychoanalytical Working Group in Frankfurt. Fromm organized the group's meetings along with Karl Landauer, Heinrich Meng, Frieda Fromm-Reichmann, and others. Fromm saw the interrelationship of psychoanalysis and sociology from the beginning in a particular way:

"The application of psychoanalysis to sociology must definitely guard against the mistake of wanting to give psychoanalytic answers where economic, technical, or political facts provide the real and sufficient explanation of sociological questions. On the other hand, the psychoanalyst must emphasize that the subject of sociology, society, in reality consists of individuals, and that it is these human beings, rather than an abstract society as such, whose actions, thoughts, and feelings are the object of sociological research."[32]

Typically, Fromm understands the individual in relation to society. The individual exists only as a related being. According to Fromm:

"Psychoanalysis interprets the human being as a socialized being, and the psychic apparatus as essentially developed and determined through the relationship of the individual to society."[33]

This definition of the individual's relationship with society, penned in 1929, contains the kernel of all that distinguishes Fromm's analytical social psychology. From the beginning, it is clear that Fromm defined his viewpoint in opposition to mainstream sociology and psychoanalysis.

A sociology that does not attempt to recognize the societal within the socialized individual was of no use to Fromm. Neither was he interested in a psychoanalysis that understands the psyche only in terms of the dynamics of drives, rather than through its social character.

Group photograph at the third Psychoanalytical Congress in Weimar, 1911. Sigmund Freud (in the center, behind the seated women); left, in front of him, Sándor Ferenczi, right, behind him Karl Landauer then, moving right in the first standing row: Carl Gustav Jung, Karl Abraham, E. Oberholzer and Wilhelm Wittenberg who analyzed Fromm in Munich.

Zeitschrift für Sozialforschung

*Zeitschrift für Sozial-forschung (*Studies in Philosophies and Social Sciences*) was the organ of the Frankfurter Schule. The table of contents of the first edition of the journal lists Fromm's article in which he declares the principles of his sociopsychological approach.*

The Committee, the inner circle around Freud in 1922, to which Fromm's last educational analyst, Hanns Sachs, (seated, right) belonged; next to him is Sándor Ferenczi. Standing, from the left, are Otto Rank, Karl Abraham, Max Eitingon, and Ernest Jones.

Fromm's main interest was in making this sociopsychological approach useful to sociology, to help understand developments in society. It was only in the middle of the 'thirties, however, that Fromm began to use this approach systematically to understand psychoanalytic theory and to bid farewell to Freud's instinct theory.

As part of his teaching program in Frankfurt, Fromm offered a course of lectures on "Psychology and Sociology" during the summer semester, in which he explained in detail his attempt to forge links between psychoanalytical thinking and a Marxist-oriented sociology.

Apart from the application of this new sociopsychological approach to questions of historic materialism, Fromm also dealt with the social psychology of religion, politics and criminal law. The focus of his interest remained the sociopsychological functionality of religious, political or criminal phenomena.

Provoked by Theodor Reik's psychoreligious work *Dogma und Zwangsidee (Dogma and Compulsion)* in which Reik sees the dogma of the crucified son of God as analogous to the rejected hatred of the individual for his father, Fromm published his first book *The Dogma of Christ* in 1930.

In it, he sees the transformation of the story of the crucified rebel—the Son of Man—into the dogma of the Son of God, as reflecting the historical development of Christians from a persecuted and suppressed minority into members of a state religion.

At the same time, this seventy-page article formulates Fromm's own sociopsychological method of survey.

IMAGO

ZEITSCHRIFT FÜR ANWENDUNG DER PSYCHOANALYSE
AUF DIE NATUR- UND GEISTESWISSENSCHAFTEN

XVI. Band   Religionspsychologisches Heft   Heft 3/4, 1930

Die Entwicklung des Christusdogmas

Eine psychoanalytische Studie
zur sozialpsychologischen Funktion der Religion

Von

Erich Fromm

I) Methodik und Problemstellung

Es ist eine der nicht unwesentlichen Leistungen der Psychoanalyse, daß
sie die falsche prinzipielle Unterscheidung zwischen einer Sozialpsychologie
und einer Psychologie des Individuums (Personalpsychologie) überwunden
hat. Freud hat einerseits betont, daß es eine Personalpsychologie, deren
Objekt der isolierte, aus dem sozialen Zusammenhang gelöste Mensch ist,

Erich Fromm's first more extensive publication in 1930: "Die Entwicklung des Christusdogmas. Eine psychoanalytische Studie zur sozialpsychologischen Funktion der Religion" ("The Development of the Dogma of Christ. A Psychoanalytical Study of the Sociopsychological Function of Religion").

"Social psychology wishes to investigate how certain attitudes common to members of a group are related to their common life experiences." It is the task of social psychology to indicate why "changes occur and how they are to be understood on the basis of the experience common to members of the group."[34]

Criminal justice and its sociopsychological function was the subject of altogether three of Fromm's publications during 1930 and 1931, as well as lectures in the winter of 1930 in Frankfurt on "The Criminal and the Punishing Society."

Be it politics, criminal justice, religion, education, or morality, Fromm always asks—as he had in his dissertation–about sociopsychological functions, explaining the group behavior of individuals through their economic and social situations and lifestyles.

In 1932 he summarized his ideas in his article "The Method and Function of an Analytical Social Psychology." In it, Fromm distinguished himself not only as a psychoanalytical social psychologist, but also largely defined the program of the Institute for Social Research (commonly known as the Frankfurt School). Fromm's article was published in the first edition of the institute's publication, the *Zeitschrift für Sozialforschung.*

Max Horkheimer–director of the Institute for Social Research–saw its main task as to explore the "dependence of the whole of so-called 'culture' on economic processes." He was convinced that this "task could not be handled successfully without the application of psycho-analytical insights."[36]

How did Fromm arrive at the Institute for Social Research? Fromm had introduced Leo Löwenthal to the Rabbi Nobel circle in Frankfurt and now, in turn, Leo Löwenthal introduced Fromm to Max Horkheimer and his disciples. Horkheimer had the idea of incorporating psychoanalysis into interdisciplinary discussions at the Institute for Social Research. He underwent a short psychoanalysis with Karl Landauer, to overcome an annoying inhibition about speaking impromptu. His experiences with psychoanalysis motivated him to afford this discipline an important place in the research plan of the institute.

The question of whether Fromm was to be appointed to oversee this also came up during Horkheimer's analysis with Landauer. Landauer himself probably

had ambitions in this direction, as he later revealed in a letter to Horkheimer: "I experienced a difficult inner struggle, when I recommended Fromm during your analysis. I would have liked to suggest that I wanted to cooperate with you."[35]

It was mainly that Fromm was able to combine psychoanalysis and historical materialism in his own sociopsychological theory, that made him an attractive candidate for the institute.

At first Fromm worked unpaid for the institute, being reimbursed only for his travel expenses between Berlin and Frankfurt.

Karl Landauer, the psychoanalyst, founded the Frankfurter Psychoanalytische Institut (Psychoanalytic Institute of Frankfurt) on the 16th of February, 1929. Cofounders were Erich Fromm, Frieda Fromm-Reichmann, and Heinrich Meng. Meng suggested inviting Fromm to work at the institute.

The Institute for Social Research in Frankfurt. It was destroyed during World War II.

The increasingly dangerous political climate in Germany in the early 'thirties led the directors of the Institute for Social Research to move their undertaking to Switzerland in 1932.

Fromm's connection with the institute solidified when he fell ill with tuberculosis and was obliged to close down his practice in Berlin. He moved to Davos in Switzerland in search of a cure. There he finally took up regular employment with the relocated institute.

1929 had marked a new departure in social research as Fromm began using psychoanalytical tools to examine the attitudes of people who saw themselves as politically left-wing.

He was principally interested in the question of whether a conscious political stance might be under-pinned by unconscious motivations. To reveal any possible contradictions between conscious thinking and unconscious drives, he used an open questionnaire and analyzed the responses.

This research was to prove controversial, as we shall see. One reason why Fromm broke with the institute in 1939 was over its lack of support for the publication of his results.

In summer 1931, Fromm fell ill for the first time with tuberculosis. From December 1932 onwards he rented a two-room apartment, number 35 in the Promenade at Davos for six months. He was able to give up the apartment only in May 1934.

At the beginning of the 'thirties Fromm was the most important source of new ideas at the institute. His sociopsychological theory and method laid the groundwork for the design of interdisciplinary research at the institute. In particular, he developed the concept of the authoritarian character in which the institute maintained an interest for over ten years. His theory and method went some way toward explaining the fascination of the petty bourgeoisie with authoritarianism and fascism.

It was these insights that brought the institute relatively early to a decision to move to Geneva in 1932–even before Hitler came to power. Shortly afterwards they transferred to Paris, then finally, in 1934, the institute found a new home at Columbia University in New York.

The move to Geneva was achieved without Fromm's assistance. In the summer of 1931 he fell ill with tuberculosis. The *Korrespondenzblatt der Internationalen Psychoanalytischen Vereinigung* (the publication of the International Psychoanalytical Association) for autumn 1931 prints a list of the extraordinary members among which appears this entry (p. 1931): "Fromm, Dr. Erich, currently in Davos. Address can be had through Dr. Frieda Fromm-Reichmann, Heidelberg, Mönchhofstr. 15."

At Davos, the first phase of Fromm's illness lasted until June 1932. Wilhelm Reich who at that time saw Fromm as an ally in his Marxist interpretation of Freud's theory of sexuality, wrote him on the 5th of June, 1932:

"Yesterday I learnt from [Barbara] Lantos, that you suffered a little relapse. This hopefully is only due to your not being careful enough! Look after yourself as much as possible. We all need you urgently."

From July 1932 Fromm was able to work for short periods at the institute in Geneva. In September, he rented a small apartment from Marie-Luise Knöpfel in the Solitudo of the Basilieri Pension in Locarno, Monti. Nevertheless his stay in Ticino was short. By the end of October 1932, Fromm was again at the Kurgarten Hotel in Davos Platz.

Johann Jakob Bachofen

Mutterrecht und Urreligion

Eine Auswahl
Herausgegeben von
Rudolf Marx

Mit einem Porträt und vier Abbildungen
Alfred Kröner Verlag / Leipzig
1 9 2 7

Dr. J J Bachofen.

Freud and Marx were vital discoveries for Fromm. In Davos, he came across another important influence on his intellectual development: Johann Jakob Bachofen. In 1861, Bachofen first determined the organization of matriarchal societies in his book *Mutterrecht und Urreligion* (*Mother Right and the Origins of Religion*) Reading this, Fromm began to question a whole range of Freud's hypotheses.

Staying at the Kurgarten Hotel was proving rather expensive. By the end of November 1932, his bill had risen to 442 Swiss Francs. So on the 1st of December, Fromm rented a two-room apartment with a roof balcony in Gustav Kraatz's house at 35, the Promenade in Davos Platz. The rent was 160 Swiss Francs. He lrented the apartment until June of the following year, by which time, he had hoped to be cured.

While he was ill, Fromm spent his time reading and developing his sociopsychological thinking. He dealt for the most part with the differences between patriarchal and matriarchal societies. He studied the texts of Bachofen, Morgan, and Briffault. "Johann Jakob Bachofen was the first to demonstrate systematically that societies are based on one of two completely different structural principles: a gynocratic, matriarchal one or a patriarchal one. In a patriarchal society, the ruling principles are the state, the law, the abstract. In the matriarchal one, they are the natural bonds."[37] In the same way, the understanding of love differs between the sexes: While a mother loves her child unconditionally, just because s/he exists, a father's love is always conditional, a love to be earned, which demands something in return.

During the 'thirties, in numerous publications and lectures, Fromm dealt with the question of the links between psychoanalysis and sociology–the sociopsychological approach to the individual as a socialized being.

Ernst Schachtel, here on a visit to Fromm in Davos, was for many years his friend and companion at the Institute for Social Research. In 1937 he married Anna Hartoch who contributed a great deal to the analysis of Fromm's "Arbeiter- und Angestelltenerhebung" (Inquiry into Workers and Employees).

Reading was often the only activity that his illness permitted; sometimes not even that was possible. As soon as he regained his strength, he wrote down his thoughts and wrote reviews for the *Zeitschrift für Sozialforschung* (*Studies in Philosophies and Social Sciences*).

He was sometimes able to receive visitors. His wife, Frieda visited him before she made an unsuccessful attempt to settle down in Palestine. Herbert Marcuse, from the institute, came on visits, as well as Ernst Schachtel who was interested in Fromm's sociopsychological research and with whom he remained on friendly terms until his death on the 28th of November, 1975.

Fromm's condition improved sufficiently for him to leave Davos (although six years later he was to suffer a relapse requiring a further stay on the Schatzalp above Davos). Paradoxically, these periods of illness were the most creative and scientifically fruitful of his life.

The first bout of sickness heralded a long separation from his wife, Frieda, and the second the no less painful separation from the Institute for Social Research, which no longer felt able to support his revision of Freudian psychoanalysis.

In autumn 1933 Fromm accepted Karen Horney's invitation to the Psychoanalytical Institute in Chicago–at that time directed by Franz Alexander. He was to give some lectures on an honorary basis. He used his stay in the United States to check out the possibility of opening an American branch of the institute or even relocating the institute there.

So Fromm made contacts in Chicago (with Harold Lasswell and John Dollard), in Boston (with Lloyd Warner and Conrad Alkon), in Philadelphia (with Bebsy Libbey, Kenneth Prey, and Caroline Newton) and in New York (with Sándor Rádo and Benjamin Stolberg). At that time, his preferred city was Philadelphia.

It is not clear if Fromm returned at the end of 1933 because of the death of his father or because of his own ill health. Until the middle of May 1934, he again lived in his apartment in Davos.

Horkheimer went to the U.S.A. in 1934 in order to follow up Fromm's contacts. Fromm gave him instructions from Davos and prepared himself for emigration.

In the middle of May 1934, Fromm stayed for a few days in the Hotel Lutétia in Paris, and on the 24th of May, he emigrated to the United States, sailing on the *George Washington* from Southampton.

4
To New Shores:
The Struggle to Define
His Own Thinking

On the 31st May, 1934, Erich Fromm arrived for a second time in America—this time as a Jewish immigrant seeking refuge from the authoritarian power of Nazism in Europe.

But this immigrant had great plans. The numerous scientific contacts Fromm had made in the autumn of 1933 in Chicago, Boston, New York, and Philadelphia promised untrammeled research opportunities and new stimuli for his sociopsychological studies of authoritarianism and the project of a social psychology rooted in historical materialism. Although his illness had allowed him little time at the Institute for Social Research in Frankfurt and Geneva, he nevertheless identified totally with its ideas and areas of research.

Contemporary correspondence with Horkheimer makes it clear how high the expectations were on both sides that, finally, they would have the opportunity to discuss and act upon the manifold political, sociopsychological, cultural-historical and philosophical ideas on their agenda. There were also several field studies that had been set up by the institute in various countries. These had to be co-ordinated, analyzed, and prepared for publication. There was never a lack of ideas or plans and Fromm could hardly wait to start discussions with Horkheimer again. The latter was five years his senior and Fromm saw him to some extent as an elder brother or father figure. Oddly, despite their regular–even intimate–correspondence, Horkheimer still addressed his younger friend as "Dear Mr. Fromm." The fact that the institute had its headquarters in the United States meant that the main actors–Horkheimer, Fromm, Marcuse, and Löwenthal–could stay in personal contact. A geographically-divided organization would inevitably have been less productive.

When Fromm arrived at the end of May 1934 in New York, Horkheimer had already been following up his leads, looking for a new base for their operations. There was a good chance that Columbia University in New York would become the institute's new home. In fact, on the 20th of July, 1934, Horkheimer was able to write Fromm that he had received a letter from the university administration confirming their "friendly anticipation of future work." The institute was to be housed at 429, West 117th Street. According to the letter, "Renovation work on the building has already started."

On the 7th of July Herbert Marcuse arrived in New York, and by the end of the month, Leo Löwenthal as well. During August, both were looking for apartments in New York City. Fromm found one first in 66th Street, before moving into an apartment overlooking Central Park in 1935.

At that time, the all-in rent was almost $100 for his new apartment–11-C at 444, Central Park West (on the corner of 104th Street). This was no small sum for a man earning $300 a month. Fromm lived there for over ten years. Horkheimer stayed in the Hotel Croydon at 86th Street until November 1938, moving only when he found a house in Scarsdale.

The fact that the members of the institute sought

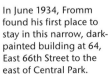

With Fromm's help, Horkheimer's search for a new home for the Institute for Social Research was successful: Columbia University in New York City made available a building in 117th Street in the summer of 1934.

In June 1934, Fromm found his first place to stay in this narrow, dark-painted building at 64, East 66th Street to the east of Central Park.

refuge in the U.S.A. was, of course, due to political developments in Germany and Europe. Although they were not practicing Jews, most of the members were of Jewish origin and worked with Karl Marx's sociology and philosophy. At least for Fromm, the hindrance of research and fear of a new war were his most important motives for emigration.

In July 1934 he wrote to Horkheimer: "I still estimate the danger of war for Europe in 1935 at 50 percent." Fromm had another, more personal, reason to emigrate: his friendship with Karen Horney. At the beginning of the 'thirties, an acquaintance with this psychoanalyst, who was fifteen years older than Fromm, grew into a friendship and then into a relationship that ended only in 1943.

[Handwritten German letter reproduced as facsimile]

Fromm's plans to make good use of his newfound freedom for research and publication were hindered by recurring bouts of illness until 1939. His extensive correspondence with Horkheimer [38] during this period owes its existence mainly to Fromm's repeated sickness, which necessitated months of recuperation. He was obliged to stay away from the institute.

As soon as he arrived in New York in 1934, his tuberculosis had become active again and he had to move to a better climate for three months. In July he stayed, with Karen Horney, at the Sunmount sanatorium, 7,500 ft. above Santa Fe in New Mexico. From there he wrote to Horkheimer: "I feel a pleasant relief after the climate of New York," and a few days later: "The air and the quiet are good for me and I am slowly starting to enjoy work again."

When, after months or weeks of recuperation, he returned to New York, he was usually able to work for only very short periods. It was with difficulty that he began to build up his psychoanalytic practice in New York and put in time for the institute, working mostly from home. His lungs needed a sea or mountain climate. Therefore Fromm went to high-altitude sanatoriums or on cruises.

The list of his journeys and stays away from New York, due to his illness during the five years he was attached to the Institute is impressive.

In the summer of 1934, he took a break of three months, staying first in Santa Fe, New Mexico, and then at the Stanley Hotel in Estes Park, Colorado, and the Hotel Broadmoor in Colorado Springs.

That winter he took a cruise

In the summer of 1934 Leo Löwenthal, a friend of Fromm's youth, also followed the Institute for Social Research to New York. This photograph from 1927 shows him together with his son David, by his wife Golde Ginsburg. At the beginning of the 'twenties, Ginsburg had been Fromm's fiancée for a while.

Herbert Marcuse also emigrated in 1934. Fromm appreciated Marcuse mainly for his philosophy. Marcuse's interpretation of Freud, however, led to sharp disagreements between the two men during the 'fifties.

on the *Empress of Britain*. From mid-1935 he stayed at Chateau Lake Louise in Alberta, Canada. There it was too cool, however, to stay and rest outside so, at the beginning of August, he traveled across Canada then through Seattle, San Francisco, and Santa Barbara to Los Angeles where he took up residence at the Hotel Del Mar. Here, too, the climate proved unfavorable, so he returned to Santa Fe and rented the Bishop's Lodge. Only in the middle of September did he return to New York. On all these stays he was accompanied by Karen Horney.

On the 19th of December, 1935, after moving into the apartment at Central Park, Fromm wrote to Hork-heimer: "I am fine, although more in my mood than in my physical condition. I have again consulted an American lung specialist, who confirmed, that my lungs are intact (which means no further development of the infection), but having had influenza twice has weaken-ed my condition and means I should stay a few more

weeks in a better climate and relax completely."

Again Fromm used the holidays at the turn of the year for recreation, this time remaining close to New York.

His bad health forced Fromm repeatedly to interrupt his work for months and seek recovery in the mountains and by the sea. He spent the turn of 1936-37 on the *M.V. Britannic* on a cruise to the West Indies and sent Horkheimer this postcard: "Dear Horkheimer, Quiet, warmth, food, wine are marvelous; besides I have read two more books in three days and this provides the necessary moral atmosphere.
With friendly greetings and thoughts,
Sincerely yours,
Erich Fromm."

In October 1935, Fromm moved into an apartment in the eleventh floor of this building at Central Park in New York City. Here he lived for almost ten years. and maintained his psychoanalytic practice.

The middle of April 1936 found Fromm on the Monarch of Bermuda, on his way to the Hotel St. George in the Bermudas. In July 1936 he made "some detours" to Mexico, where he stayed in Señorita Scott's house in the mountains of Taxco, visited Acapulco, and met Otto Rühle.

After his return in the middle of September 1936 he fell ill again; then his mother came for a visit for a few weeks. On the night of the 19th December, 1936, he started another cruise on the M. V. *Britannic* to the West Indies. In a letter to Karl Landauer, Horkheimer observed that "Fromm has already covered half the continent."

On the 2nd of July, 1937, Fromm left New York, leaving his car, a Tudor Ford Sedan, to Leo Löwenthal (who lived on 111th Street) and traveled with Karen Horney to the mountains near Tahoe City in California on the Nevada border.

Fromm gave up his original plan to spent a second summer in Taxco, Mexico, where he had hoped to meet Otto Rühle again. Instead, Anna Hartoch and Ernst Schachtel (his most important supporters in analyzing his study of workers and employees) came to visit for two weeks. In November 1937 these two were married.

When Fromm returned to New York at the beginning of September 1937 he came down with influenza and was afterwards plagued for weeks with kidney inflammation. On the 29th of December, he let Otto Rühle know:

"My health is unfortunately still not good. My kidney inflammation has not disappeared yet and I will have to interrupt my work after New Year and rest for four weeks."

On the 25th of February, 1938, Fromm was on the move again, this time in a Pullman compartment of the Pennsylvania Railroad on the way to Litchfield Park in Arizona. There he spent a month in a bungalow of the Hotel Wigwam on the edge of the desert. Meanwhile, Horkheimer wrote impatiently to Karl Landauer on the 7th of March, that Fromm still had not returned and "is staying at a beautiful place in Arizona, a few days' journey from here."

What seems to be an outrageous travel compulsion, was in reality a desperate attempt to overcome an illness that upset Fromm's plans again and again and that made his life very insecure. Additionally, the political situation depressed him ever more. Hitler's continual striving to expand Germany's borders, fascism in Italy, the Spanish civil war and Franco's victory, the terror regime of Stalin, the show trials in Moscow, and the annexation of Austria in March 1938–all this took a toll on Fromm.

"It looks horrific in the world," he wrote on the 29th of December, 1937 to Otto Rühle in Mexico. And to Horkheimer, in a letter at the end of February 1938 from Arizona: "All the political news of the last few weeks has been worse then ever; the news about the new trials in Moscow is horrifying."

During his stay in Europe in the summer of 1938, Fromm fell ill again with tuberculosis. He was forced to stay on the

Schatzalp above Davos in Switzerland until the beginning of February 1939.

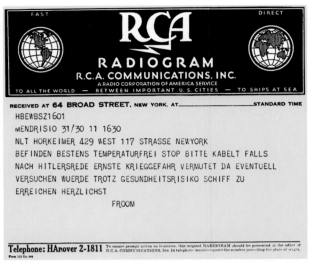

FAST   DIRECT

RCA
RADIOGRAM
R.C.A. COMMUNICATIONS, INC.
A RADIO CORPORATION OF AMERICA SERVICE
TO ALL THE WORLD — BETWEEN IMPORTANT U. S. CITIES — TO SHIPS AT SEA

RECEIVED AT 64 BROAD STREET, NEW YORK, AT_____STANDARD TIME
HBEWBSZ1601
MENDRISIO 31/30 11 1630
NLT HORKEIMER 429 WEST 117 STRASSE NEWYORK
BEFINDEN BESTENS TEMPERATURFREI STOP BITTE KABELT FALLS
NACH HITLERSREDE ERNSTE KRIEGGEFAHR VERMUTET DA EVENTUELL
VERSUCHEN WUERDE TROTZ GESUNDHEITSRISIKO SCHIFF ZU
ERREICHEN HERZLICHST
FROOM

Telephone: HAnover 2-1811   To secure prompt action on inquiries, this original RADIOGRAM should be presented at the office of R.C.A. COMMUNICATIONS, Inc. In telephone inquiries quote the number preceding the place of origin.

His illness was at first diagnosed as scarlet fever. After the fever was over, Fromm send this telegram to Horkheimer in New York on the 12th of September, 1938.

A few months later, he fought his last major battle with tuberculosis. At the beginning of July 1938, Fromm had traveled to Europe again for the first time since 1934. He was accompanied by Karen Horney. They spent a few weeks in Paris, on the Loire, then in the Riviera. On the 1st of September, 1938, he cabled Horkheimer from Ospedale Cantonale in Mendrisio in Southern Switzerland: "Have fallen ill with scarlet fever–return in about two months." Only after he had been transferred to the San Rocco sanatorium in Lugano was the diagnosis found to be wrong. Fromm had actually succumbed to tuberculosis again.

Along with the illness, his fear of war increased considerably. Hitler pursued his claim to the Sudentenland in Czechoslovakia ever more boldly, finally achieving his goal at the end of September with the Munich Agreement.

Even before the diagnosis was clear, Fromm cabled Horkheimer on the 12th of September, 1938 that he wanted to use his temporary freedom from fever to get on a ship, in order to leave war-threatened Europe. Horkheimer considered "war, with France and Germany on different sides for the next years not very

likely" (in a letter to Fromm dated the 16th of September).

So once again Fromm had to spend several months on the Schatzalp above Davos hoping to cure his tuberculosis. Depressed by the illness and by political developments, he wrote Horkheimer on the 4th of November: "Yes it has been a bit too much these last two months, especially regarding what's happening in the world and the horrifying individual misery, which you come across in newspapers and letters. Sometimes, during these weeks, it has seemed more than doubtful to me if, under the circumstances, it was still worth holding on to one's life as it were 'by force,' through doctors, medicines—and the inner will to live. But the feeling 'I can make it' stayed more prominent.

Ever fewer people remain who are neither enthusiastic nor numbed by events. But we have a responsibility as individuals not to give in. Besides this there is satisfaction in knowing that, even though we might get physically crushed by the steamroller of historical events, we will still stay intact spiritually and morally."

On top of illness and the political threat came other

worries: Fromm had no money to finance his mother's emigration to England (the institute had paid for his doctors and his stay in the sanatorium), and he was worried that staying away more than six months from the U.S.A. could jeopardize his naturalization.

In the end, his fears proved unfounded: On the 22nd of December Fromm ended a letter to Horkheimer with the following words: "But now, that I know I will travel in about four weeks, I am full of joy. My health is improving all the time and the doctor promises me that in four weeks my lungs will be better than they have been for five years. My kidneys are fine again and I am beginning to feel like someone who can use his strength once more." At the beginning of February 1939, Fromm returned on the *Normandie* to New York. Thanks to newly developed drugs, he was now cured of tuberculosis once and for all.

At the end of his stay on the Schatzalp in Davos, Fromm was pronounced cured thanks to progress made in medication for tuberculosis.

Despite Fromm's numerous illnesses between 1931 and 1939, his work for the Institute for Social Research continued, and he contributed to discussions of what were later called the critical theories.

His principal contributions to sociopsychological theory and method in 1932 in the *Zeitschrift für Sozialforschung* and the first psychoanalytic field research among German workers and employees (1929-30) have already been mentioned.

Fromm's reading during his periods of illness and recuperation led to numerous reviews and further articles for the *Zeitschrift für Sozialforschung*. Notable are his articles on *Mother Right* (1933 and 1934), a sociopsychological critique of Freud's therapy (1935), and *Zum Gefühl der Ohnmacht* (*The Feeling of Impotence*) (1937).

The main focus of his work from 1934 onwards was to describe the authoritarian character—then known as the "sadomasochistic character." With this, Fromm, created the sociopsychological basis for *Studien über Autorität und Familie* (*Studies on Authority and Family*) in 1936 and the theoretical concept for the numerous investigations into authority that the institute carried out during the 'thirties and that Fromm undertook to coordinate and publish.

After finishing the sociopsychological section of *Studies on Authority and Family* in the end of 1935, Fromm started, with Horkheimer's approval, to write a book about the bourgeois character. In the spring of 1937, the work had to be interrupted for two years not only because of his illness, but also because he tried to revise psychoanalytic theory in an article that drew criticism from other members of the institute. It was not until 1941 that the book was published, after extensive revisions, under the title *Escape from Freedom*.

Between 1935 and 1938, he spent most of his time analyzing the research on workers and employees that the institute had conducted in 1929 and 1930. Fromm's decision to analyze and prepare it for publication came only at the end of 1935, when he examined forty selected questionnaires and came to the conclusion "that it is worthwhile in the common scientific interest and specifically in the interest of the institute to do the work." (Letter to Horkheimer dated the 10th of January 1936).

Fromm strengthened his contacts with the Sarah Lawrence College in Bronxville at the same time. From the summer of 1936 onwards, he conducted research with students of the college on how the process of learning was influenced by their different attitudes toward authority.

Table from the study of workers and employees regarding question No. 431: "Who do you think was responsible for hyperinflation"?

Table

Answer Categories	Question: Who, in your opinion, was to blame for the inflation?												
	Social Democrats				Left Social Demo.	Communists				B-Vot.	Nat. Soo.	Non Vot.	Total
	1	2	3	Total		1	2	3	Total				
1 Capitalism	31	15	24	21	36	56	28	45	42	2	6	15	26
2 Big industrialists or landowners	3	4	8	4	-	3	13	-	8	2	-	-	4
3 Banks, stock exchange	2	5	3	3	2	8	3	11	5	2	6	2	4
4 Government	11	9	10	10	12	7	13	11	10	12	6	15	10
5 Other nations	15	22	20	20	28	8	8	11	8	7	6	16	16
6 Individual Persons (Schacht)	10	6	14	9	4	2	5	-	3	10	32	4	7
7 Jews	-	1	1	1	-	-	-	-	-	8	25	3	2
8 Miscellaneous	6	12	2	8	11	-	9	-	5	28	6	8	9
9 Unanswered	23	26	20	24	7	16	21	22	19	18	13	37	22
Total %	100	100	100	100	100	100	100	100	100	100	100	100	100

Fromm's idea of subjecting his research on workers and employees to psychoanalytic analysis was innovative. The freely given responses to 270 questions were treated as if they were the words of patients on the couch. Fromm wanted to check for a coherent pattern of contradictions, thereby to reveal his subjects' unconscious attitudes and character traits. He was especially interested in comparing unconscious conflicts with conscious political attitudes. Processing over 600 questionnaires, however, proved an almost unmanageable task. Particularly difficult was the classification of the hidden conflicts he discovered, and relating them to specific personality types.

In his statistical work, Fromm collaborated with Paul F. Lazarsfeld, with whom he was on friendly terms. The psychoanalytic analysis was done with Ernst Schachtel, Anna Hartoch, and Herta Herzog—Lazarsfeld's wife. Hilde Weiß coordinated everything and wrote a preliminary report.

50 years later, Herta Herzog still remembers the meetings in Fromm's Bauhaus-style flat. The meetings usually ended with a good meal, which Fromm had arranged. The air was always saturated with his cigar smoke and while relaxing they would often listen to Hasidic music from his record collection.[39]

The result of the study was impressive: all subjects declared themselves to be politically left-wing, but only in 15 percent of cases did this conscious position accord with an unconscious revolutionary personality structure. In a further 15 percent, the unconscious character orientation proved to be reactionary, while the majority—70 percent—revealed a hidden ambivalence and therefore remained open to a fascist or national socialist agenda. He already interpreted "the discrepancy between their conscious leftist political opinions and the underlying personality structure as possibly responsible for the collapse of the German workers' parties."[40]

In his letters from the years 1936 to 1938, Fromm
repeatedly mentioned how much time and energy he
had invested in the analysis of this study. On the 31st of
December, 1937 he wrote to Gustav Bally in
Switzerland: "With 600 questionnaires each six pages
long, being able to extract anything of quality was a
great deal of work, much more than I had anticipated.
Now it is almost finished and will soon be published in
English."

Shortly before Fromm went to Europe in June 1938
he was in a position to offer the manuscript to a New
York publisher.

It did not get published then, however. Horkheimer
showed ambivalence toward the research.

"(Horkheimer) originally was hesitant to agree to
its being done but then agreed and when he read it at
first, he declared that he found it extremely valuable
and important." But on Fromm's return from
Switzerland in February 1939, "he said that it could not
be published because the Institute had no money for
publication." [41]

Herbert Marcuse in 1937

Back in New York in February 1939 Fromm had recovered his physical health. His position at the institute was less sound, however. In May 1939, Friedrich Pollock, the financial manager, told him that the institute could no longer afford to pay his salary after October of that year and he would have to leave.

The institute had in fact suffered serious losses on its investments. Furthermore, Fromm's contribution to the institute had diminished due to his prolonged illness.

The decision to cancel a lifelong contract with the institute's main source of ideas and to compensate him with $4,000—one year's salary, can be understood only by considering the special relationship between Fromm and Horkheimer and the influence that Theodor Wiesengrund Adorno had on the institute from 1937 onwards.

The mutual appreciation between Fromm and Horkheimer was unusually idealizing. This led, after the breakup, to a lasting mutual denigration. Both had excessively high expectations of one other, which they expressed repeatedly in letters. The alienation began with Fromm's questioning of Freud's libido theory.

In the beginning of the 'thirties, he had tried to formulate a connection between individual psychological structures and society with the help of the Freudian libido theory and developed the concept of a libidinous structure of society.

Revolutionary research into matriarchy and the results of cultural-anthropological studies by Margaret Mead, Ruth Benedict, and others, convinced Fromm that those urges that characterize human behavior are not adequately explained by instincts alone. Fromm's close scientific and personal relationship with Karen Horney reinforced this view. Instincts, in the Freudian sense, develop according to their own inherent dynamics. They are genetically inherited and manifest themselves in attachments to the body's erogenous zones.

In a letter on the 1st of June, 1936, Fromm writes: "The task seems to me to be to understand the structures of character and instincts as a result of adaptation to the given social conditions and not as a product of the erogenous zones." Horkheimer saw in Freud's instincts the materialistic basis for physical phenomena.

But Fromm criticized Freud's instinct-based psychology specifically in this respect: "[to look at] man as an animal coerced by his instincts but domesticated by society. He lacks all categories of spontaneity, such as love, tenderness, joy and even sexual pleasure as far as it is more than relief from tension." [42]

For Fromm, too, instincts play an important role in the lives of human beings but "those emotions which essentially motivate human action are historically (socially) conditioned." [42]

"Psychoanalysis—the enigma of the unconscious"–a suggestion for a poster for a film (which was never made) about psychoanalysis in the 'twenties.

Fromm wrote first to his colleague at the institute, Karl August Wittfogel, who was in China at that time, about his "quite fundamental" reexamination of Freud.

Fromm had to reformulate his own approach without the help of Freud's instinct theory. In autumn 1936 he started to write the article in which he explained his differences with Freud.

On the 18th of December 1936, he wrote to his colleague from the institute, Karl August Wittfogel, who was in China at that time: "Unfortunately I have started to think and write again about problems which I thought had been solved. I worked over my fundamental reexamination of Freud. The core of the argument is when I try to demonstrate that those urges which motivate social activities are not, as Freud supposes, sublimations of sexual instincts, rather products of social processes or, to be more precise, reactions to certain circumstances in which human beings need to satisfy their instincts. These urges differ in principle from the natural factors, namely the drives to satisfy hunger, thirst and sexual desire. While all human beings and animals have these in common, the others are specifically human productions. The problem within psychology and sociology is the dialectic intertwining of natural and historical factors. Freud has wrongly based psychology totally on natural factors."

By the summer of 1937, Fromm's fundamental reexamination was ready to be discussed by the institute for publication in the *Zeitschrift für Sozialforschung*. Apparently, his attempt to formulate a

psychoanalytic theory that differed from Freud provoked broad resistance–not only from Horkheimer. On the 10th of September, 1937, Fromm wrote to Horkheimer, that he therefore wanted to rework the article thoroughly, but that he was "still convinced, that the main idea is right."

The "main idea" which Fromm developed here and which remained decisive for the whole of his further thinking can be gathered in three hypotheses:

1. "We arrive at two elements in the psychic structure which must be differentiated: the naturally given physiological drives and the historical psychic impulses, developed in the social process."

2. "The life process, in which [a man's] physiological needs are but an aspect, and not his physiology, forms the material basis by which his psychic structure can be understood."

3. "The differences in the manner of production and life of various societies or classes lead to the development of different character structures typical for a particular society."[43]

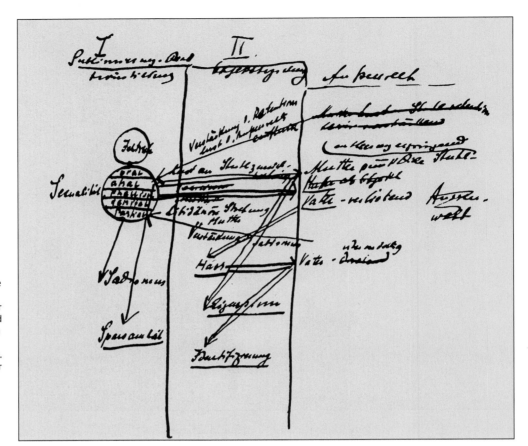

In Fromm's 1937 article, this handwritten sketch was meant to illustrate the two kinds of drive, differentiated here for the first time.

The reactions listed under I are understood by Freud as springing directly from sexuality, modified by environmental influences. The reactions listed under II are, according to Fromm, object relationships. These are not direct products of sexuality but reactions to the environment.

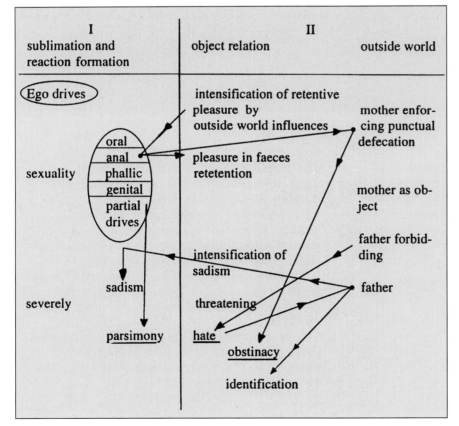

This new approach enabled new insights into the passionate strivings of human beings. Since action is no longer determined by instinct but by economic and societal imperatives, it becomes clear why, in authoritarian systems, sadism and masochism are dominant drives. Fromm demonstrated the fertility and modernity of his approach, not only with his research into the authoritarian character, but also with his later studies into the "marketing character" and the necrophilic orientation.

The current omnipresent desire always to be a success, or the widespread tendency to calculate everything as if it were a dead thing cannot be explained, fatalistically, as a predetermined outcome of inherent instincts, developed during early childhood, rather

as an internalization of an economy and society oriented toward marketing or toward the reification of everything.

This reification is difficult to explain away as determined from their earliest childhood. It is rather a result of the particular orientation of the society and economy in which they live: an orientation that reduces everything to the material level.

Fromm was aware that this different approach meant an attack on orthodox psychoanalytic instinct theory, since "according to the theory here suggested the psychic structure of man is regarded as the product of his activity and his manner of life and not as the reflex thrown up by his physical organization." [43] He did not, however, expect rejection by his institute colleagues, because he thought, quite reasonably, that his new approach accorded with the ideas of historical materialism.

The fact is that, from first acquaintance, Fromm had developed a marked aversion to Theodor Wiesengrund Adorno. Unfortunately, Adorno's influence on the theoretical thinking of Horkheimer, Löwenthal, and Pollock was considerable. Indeed, Adorno was a prime mover in the rejection of Fromm's new approach. Fromm was aware of this, writing that the reason the

institute defended orthodox psychoanalysis against him "partly had to do with the influence of Adorno, whom from the very beginning of his appearance in New York I criticized very sharply." [44]

Adorno tried systematically to undermine Horkheimer's connection with Fromm. In March 1936 "Teddy Wiesengrund" was already criticizing Fromm's 1935 paper "Die gesellschafliche Bedingtheit der psychoanalytischen Therapie" (The Social determination of Psychoanalytic Therapy) in a letter to Horkheimer:

"This time I did not like Fromm at all—he put me into the paradoxical situation of defending Freud." In February 1937, Horkheimer invited Adorno to become an employee of the Institute. Adorno reacted with criticism of Fromm's position at the institute and wrote back on the 23rd of March: "The position occupied by Fromm is of greatest importance: that is why I think he has to be particularly careful not to put psychology and society on the same level in an Adlerian sense. I find traces of this in the article ("Zum Gefühl der Ohnmacht," "On the Feeling of Impotence," 1937).

Controversy broke out in the Institute for Social Research over the search for the unconscious. Fromm freed Freud's psychoanalysis from its basis in instinct theory and proposed a new sociopsychological approach. This made a different understanding of the unconscious possible—not only the unconscious of individuals but also of society.

Horkheimer answered Adorno on the 6th of April, 1937: "Despite all fine psychological descriptions by Fromm there is the danger of sliding into revisionism. This is also being discussed here. Fromm is explaining his position these days in our lectures at Columbia University. Your reaction corresponds exactly with my objections." On the 23rd of April, 1937, Adorno reassured himself about this agreement with Horkheimer: " I am glad that we share the same instinct about Fromm's article."

On the 18th of July, shortly before Fromm's "Fundamental Essay" failed at the institute, Horkheimer wrote to Adorno, that he shared his joy about Adorno's officially joining the institute: "In order to complete the task of developing the theory we really do need you."

Fromm's new approach and Adorno's arrival at the institute in the summer of 1937 already point in the direction of Fromm's departure. In 1939 the break was arranged, under the pretext of lack of money. Fromm described the change in his relationship with Horkheimer in a memorandum in November of that year: "Since a few years Dr. Horkheimer has changed his attitude to my work. He accused me of being a conformist and that my theoretical approach was not particularly fruitful any more for the use of psychology in the social sciences. In general, he expressed his opinion at different times that psychology was only of minor importance for social science anyway. This is in strict contradiction to his attitude prior to that time."[41]

Looking back, Fromm's departure seems like the beginning of the end for the Institute for Social Research. He was not the only victim of financial difficulties and new politics of the institute, Julian Gumperz, who had been employed since 1934 and advised the institute on financial matters, was asked to leave. Now Karl August Wittfogel left and, finally, Hendryk Grossmann and Franz Neumann. Deprived of the means to support their research, the "survivors" were forced to scale down the institute and eventually to close it.

Psychoanalysis of society deals with the social unconscious of the individual as a socialized being.

The alienation between Horkheimer and Fromm and the accompanying mutual denigration was never overcome. For Horkheimer, Fromm was the "only serious disappointment," as he wrote to Felix Weil on the 20th of March, 1942. Though Fromm never made any move against the institute, Horkheimer had a paranoid fear that Fromm might set up a front against the institute together with Gumperz, Wittfogel, Robert Lynd, and others.

Regarding his evaluation of psychoanalysis, Horkeimer maintained his view that: "Psychology without libido is no psychology. Where psychology is needed, we have to refer in an orthodox way to Freud's earlier writings. Freud (by developing the concept of the death instinct) objectively absented himself from psychoanalysis, whereas Fromm and Horney get back to a 'commonsense psychology' and even psychologize culture and society." [45]

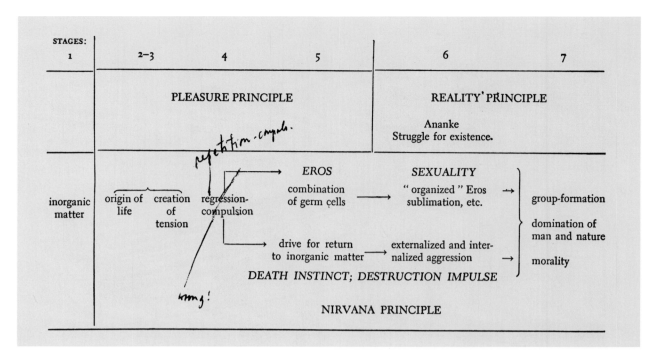

STAGES:						
1	2–3	4	5		6	7

It was not without some satisfaction that Fromm jumped on this revealing printing error in a diagram in Marcuse's 1955 *Eros and Civilization*. Fromm criticized Marcuse for his use of Freud as an advocate for a liberating regression to polymorphous sexuality. He corrected "regression compulsion" to "repetition compulsion."

Revising his theory in 1920, Freud had conceived of two continually warring instincts: the life and death instincts. He implied that there is a never-ending dichotomy between these basic urges and the ideals of culture. Adorno believed that, by abandoning this theory, Fromm was seeking to deny this basic dichotomy and was thus ignoring the negative dialectic between drive and society. Fromm was accused of arriving at his positive position by neglecting the death instinct as a primary natural fact.

In a lecture on the 26th of April, 1946, in Los Angeles, Adorno stated for the first time in public that the rejection of Freud's libido psychology led in reality to the denial of "culture which imposes restrictions on libidinous and specifically on destructive drives, contributing to the development of repression, guilt feelings and the urge for self punishment."[46]

Of course, Fromm had never doubted that culture had two faces. To maintain that society shapes an individual's psychological structure in no way requires that the destructiveness of society be played down or even denied.

While it is true that Fromm avoided dualism and the concept of a hopeless struggle between drive claim and culture, he attributed the final responsibility for destructive behavior not to the inherent dynamic of drives, but to the historical conditioning of mankind. For Fromm, man has an opportunity to develop his capacity for love; only if this fails, does he turn to destructive behavior. The label "revisionist" was often bandied about. Even today, an outrageously clichéd critique of Fromm is being repeated by Adorno's, Marcuse's, and Horkheimer's followers, treating as dogma what Horkheimer wrote to the publishers of the

After Fromm left the Institute for Social Research, Herbert Marcuse was the only former colleague with whom Fromm still had dealings (although these were often controversial). This photograph from the 'thirties shows Herbert Marcuse (left, with his arm in plaster), Erich Fromm (right), and in the center Juliette Favez, the secretary of the Institute for Social Research's Geneva office.

Philosophical Review in April 1949: "Fromm left the institute and became the head of one of the 'revisionist' schools of psychoanalysis that has tried to 'sociologize' deep psychology, thereby, as some of my associates and I felt, actually making it more superficial and losing sight of the decisive social implications of Freud's original conception." Much later, Fromm reacted by denigrating Horkheimer. He wrote on the 28th of July, 1975 to Raya Dunayevskaya, an American Marxist and the former secretary of Leon Trotsky, about the members of the institute: "These people, particularly Horkheimer, became so frightened after they had come to America of being considered radicals that they began first to suppress all words which sounded radical, and Horkheimer eventually ended [up] as a pillar of society in Frankfurt, praising religion and the virtues of capitalism."

The only one with whom Fromm later maintained a relationship was Herbert Marcuse. This relationship was, however, ambivalent since Fromm dealt critically with Marcuse's work. He wrote in another letter to Raya Dunayevskaya on the 31st of July, 1968: "After having read the whole of *One-Dimensional Man* and *Eros and Civilization* I am really shocked, not only about the incompetent treatment of Freud, which is a drastic distortion, but more than that about the irrational and, to me, somewhat sickening character of his ideas for the future man. Excellent as Marcuse is with his purely philosophical work, these two books are the expression of an alienation and despair masquerading as radicalism. Basically his 'salvation' lies in regression to infantile egotism, and as far as the polymorphous sexuality is concerned, I don't think we need a revolution for that."

5
Venture of Freedom: The New Identity

The end of Fromm's cooperation with the Institute for Social Research (Institut für Sozialforschung) mainly had to do with a new psychoanalytic approach that Fromm developed during the middle of the 'thirties. This innovative, creative approach made the "socialized person" its point of reference. Fromm maintained that the psychological structure of such a person does not develop according to the inherent dynamics of drives, but develops from experience and adapts by being related to reality. This notion fell on stony ground at the institute, but was positively received by others and led to new contacts.

One such was the psychoanalyst Karen Horney, Fromm's friend for twelve years and a constant travel companion. Horney was fifteen years older than Fromm and helped a great deal in developing his new psychoanalytic approach.

Fromm met Karen Horney through Georg Groddeck in Baden Baden and they became better acquainted during his studies at the psychoanalytic institute in Berlin. Horney had invited him to Chicago in 1933. Both were interested in the influence of societies and cultures on the human psyche. They also believed that the role of the basic drives which Freud associated with numerous psychological phenomena needed to be revised. Together they applied Bachofen's, Briffault's, and Morgan's concepts of the maternal and paternal social structures along with ideas from comparative cultural anthropology. Both of them had no doubt that Freud's views of human nature, women, the Oedipus Complex, penis envy, etc. had sociocultural origins. For them Freud's views demonstrated a patriarchal

approach to human nature and had to be revised. It was not to be expected that Fromm's new psychoanalytic theories would be taken up by orthodox psychoanalysts.

Gustav Bally in Zurich, however, welcomed Fromm's attempt, in a letter on the 8th of December, 1936, in the following words: "It is not the fact that you distance yourself from Freud's theory of the libido, but the manner in which you do so that meets with my entire approval. I do not think that this theory is a shibboleth or key concept of psychoanalysis, rather it is one of those physical-mechanistic skins, which need to be shed so one can develop further."

Karen Horney, who lived in the U.S.A. from 1932, and Erich Fromm made contact with a wide range of people interested in the psychological influences of society and culture. Among them were Margaret Mead, Ruth Benedict, John Dollard, Harold D. Lasswell, and Abram Kardiner. Kardiner remembers the evenings with Dollard and Fromm in Horney's hotel apartment, where they played roulette while Fromm sang "Hasidic songs in a beautiful and soulful voice." [47]

Vital feedback for Fromm's new theory came from Harry Stack Sullivan. It led in the following years to a new field of activity within psychological theory and practice. On the 21st of October, 1936, Fromm received an invitation from Sullivan, who was president of the William Alanson White Psychoanalytic Foundation, to lecture at the new Washington School of Psychiatry in Washington.

Fromm was enthusiastic about the program of the Washington School of Psychiatry. Students of medicine, anthropology, psychology, and related disciplines were to be educated in psychiatry and connected studies. The human being was to be approached as a "psychobiological organism, social in orientation."

Sullivan's invitation to lecture at the Washington School of Psychiatry. This letter, perhaps the most important he received in the 'thirties, secured Fromm's future as a psychoanalyst .

This private psychiatric clinic, Chestnut Lodge in Rockville near Washington D.C., became the center of the new interpersonal psychoanalysis.

Fromm wrote back on the 27th of October, 1939: "May I express my congratulations [on] your plans. The school promises to become a new beginning and a center of a psychiatry and of psychoanalytic theory, freed from the shackles of sterile dogmatism and fertile through being rooted in the soil of an understanding of culture and social dynamics."

Harry Stack Sullivan (1892-1949) had become familiar with psychiatry through the urging of William Alanson White (1870-37). He tried to understand schizophrenic illnesses through Freud's insights, but using new techniques. He modified the classical method, which focused all efforts on reconstructing the destroyed Ego. Sullivan considered that the most important means of enabling the schizophrenic to reestablish contact with the outer world was face-to-face communication dealing with the patient's daily problems and offering, above all, emotional attention and warmth.

In 1928, Sullivan had pressured Clara Thompson to be analyzed by Ferenczi. He then underwent a didactic analysis himself with Clara Thompson. From 1930, he practiced in Washington as well as in New York. His first contact with Fromm probably came through Clara Thompson, because, in 1934, she continued with Fromm the analysis that had begun with Ferenczi.

The "Theory of Interpersonal Relationships" united Sullivan and Fromm. This theory made it much easier to understand Fromm's own new psychoanalytic ideas than did Freud's libido theory. In *Escape from Freedom* (1941) Fromm wrote a few years later: "We believe that man is primarily a social being, and not, as Freud assumes, primarily self-sufficient and only secondarily in need of others in order to satisfy his instinctual needs. In this sense, we believe that individual psychology is fundamentally social psychology or, in Sullivan's terms, the psychology of interpersonal relationships; the key problem of psychology is that of the particular kind of relatedness of the individual toward the world, not that of satisfaction or frustration of single instinctual desires."[48]

Sullivan's invitation to Fromm in 1936 to cooperate in the Washington School of Psychiatry did not come as a total surprise, but was the result of Fromm's contacts with Clara Thompson and with Frieda Fromm-Reichmann,

Harry Stack Sullivan had excellent results with his new method of handling patients. He explained this by noting that the basic problem of the human being is his or her relationship with reality, especially with other people. According to Sullivan, psychiatry should become the "science of human relationships."

HARRY STACK SULLIVAN, M.D.

THE

Interpersonal Theory
of Psychiatry

Edited by
HELEN SWICK PERRY *and* MARY LADD GAWEL
With an Introduction by MABEL BLAKE COHEN, M.D.

W·W·NORTON & COMPANY·INC·*New York*

From the beginning, Sullivan put into effect the concept that even a serious severe pathological clinical picture is usually the sign of some disturbance in the relationship with reality as opposed to a frustrated drive. He favored a theory of relationships over one of instincts.

his first wife. Clara Thompson was the first president of the Washington-Baltimore Psychoanalytic Society, of which Sullivan was a cofounder. Until 1939, she commuted between New York and Washington to lecture. Fromm did the same, along with Sullivan, Horney, and William Silverberg who had returned from Berlin in 1933.

After she finished the second part of her didactical analysis in 1935, Thompson became a member of the New York Psychoanalytic Society. Her warm relationship with Fromm held up through all confusions and splits of the psychoanalytic societies during the 'forties.

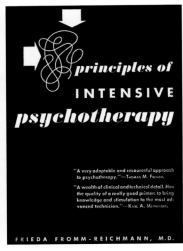

principles of

INTENSIVE

psychotherapy

"A very adaptable and resourceful approach to psychotherapy."—THOMAS M. FRENCH.

"A wealth of clinical and technical detail. Has the quality of a really good primer; to bring knowledge and stimulation to the most advanced technician."—KARL A. MENNINGER.

FRIEDA FROMM-REICHMANN, M.D.

In her book *Principles of Intensive Psychotherapy*, Frieda Fromm-Reichmann made clear her special way of dealing with patients. Students of Erich Fromm may also read here of how far he reshaped the therapeutic relationship.

The Frieda Fromm-Reichmann Cottage in the park at Chestnut Lodge still reminds us of her therapeutic work. She remained an active therapist there until her death in 1957.

Frieda-Fromm Reichmann knew Sullivan through lectures that he held at Chestnut Lodge, the psychiatric clinic in Rockeville not far from Washington. She arrived there more by chance then by design. She had escaped the pressure of the Nazis and moved her practice to Strasbourg on the 1st of July, 1933. In 1934 she went to Palestine for six months and finally emigrated to the U.S.A. in 1935.

What was intended to be a two months' temporary position, substituting for a vacationing member of staff at Chestnut Lodge, became an engagement lasting twenty-two years, years which proved very beneficial for those suffering from psychotic illnesses. Her reputation spread throughout the world.

This international reputation was boosted by Hannah Green's best-selling autobiography *I Never Promised you a Rose Garden*, later made into a film. In this book, a patient details how a "Dr. Fried" helped her recover from schizophrenia. "Dr. Fried" was in reality Frieda Fromm-Reichmann.

Besides Hannah Green's story, there are few descriptions of Frieda Fromm-Reichmann as a therapist. One of her students, however, writes of her: "She was loved and feared by her students in the same time. She was loved because of her warmth, empathy, and insight toward everybody, and feared because of her sharp observation of the neurotic negative counter-transference reactions of psychoanalytic students during their work with patients."[49]

Frieda Fromm-Reichmann owes a lot to Sullivan's insights and urging in her therapeutic work with schizophrenic patients. She gives her own view of this work in her book *Principles of Intensive*

Psychotherapy.[50] A comparison of her account with those of Sullivan, Thompson, and Fromm demonstrates the influence of Sullivan and Ferenczi on her work.

For Erich Fromm, contact with Sullivan meant a new beginning in various ways. To some extent, Sullivan's theory of Interpersonal Psychoanalysis formed a useful metapsychological framework for Fromm's new approach to psychoanalysis. At the same time it provided a spiritual home for his own psychoanalytic theory and a new field of activity.

For Fromm, the active therapist, contact with Sullivan and the Washington School of Psychiatry brought with it feelings of identification and belonging.

Sullivan's experiences of therapy were broadly similar to those that Fromm, Fromm-Reichmann, Horney, and Thompson came to know through Groddeck, and Ferenczi and which, to varying degrees, they put into practice.

They all agreed not to position themselves as therapists using Freud's ideal model of the neutral observer. Observation of patients does not imply objective distance, rather it involves taking part on a human level. Observation can "become understanding only to the extent that the observer understands his participation, without just neutralizing it coolly and objectively."[51]

Frieda Fromm-Reichmann, who lived apart from Erich Fromm after 1931, came to Chestnut Lodge in 1935. With the book *I Never Promised You a Rose Garden*, a patient, Hannah Green, brought her international fame as the first woman successfully to treat schizophrenic patients through psychoanalysis.

During the middle of the 'thirties, Fromm made a breakthrough in his own psychoanalytic approach and in his own identity as a therapist. Fromm documented both developments. Curiously enough, he made no effort to bring either of these important papers to attention. The "Fundamental Essay", which he wrote in 1937, was rejected by his collegues at the Institute for Social Research. Although he later extended it, the paper was never published.

Another essay, "Die gesellschaftliche Bedingtheit der psychoanalytischen Therapie," (The Social Determination of Psychoanalytic Therapy) in which he deals in detail with the role of the therapist, was published in 1935. Even today, apart from the German original, there exists only one translation—into Italian.

It shows very clearly how Fromm distanced himself from Freud's recommendations about psychoanalytic technique and his argument in favor of dealing with patients using the methods of Georg Groddeck and Sándor Ferenczi.

Although Fromm repeatedly planned to write down his own ideas on therapeutic technique, the results were rudimentary, contributing to the fact that his own approach is virtually unknown and rarely applied today.

In "Die gesellschaftliche Bedingtheit der psychoanalytischen Therapie" Fromm deals mainly with Freud's short *Ratschläge für den Arzt bei der psychoanalytischen Behandlung* (*Recommendations to Physicians PractisingPsychoanalysis*), 1912 and his *Bemerkungen über die Übertragungsliebe* (*Observations on Transference-Love*), 1915.

Die gesellschaftliche Bedingtheit der psychoanalytischen Therapie.

Von
Erich Fromm.

Die psychoanalytische Therapie beruht auf der Aufdeckung der zur Symptombildung oder zur Bildung neurotischer Charaktereigenschaften führenden unbewussten Strebungen. Die Symptome sind Ausdruck des Konflikts zwischen solchen unbewussten verdrängten und den sie verdrängenden Tendenzen. Die wichtigste Ursache der Verdrängung ist die Angst. Ursprünglich und zunächst einmal die Angst vor äusserer Gewalt, die aber, soll eine wirksame Verdrängung zustande kommen, ergänzt wird durch die Angst, Sympathie und Liebe derjenigen zu verlieren, die man respektiert und bewundert, und endlich durch die Angst vor dem Verlust des Respekts vor sich selbst[1]). Allerdings ist auch die Angst vor dem Verlust der Liebe einer bewunderten Person gewöhn-

With this essay in 1935, Fromm declared himself for Groddeck's and Ferenczi's "humane" therapeutic approach. At the same time he distanced himself from Freud's "patricentric-authoritarian" ideas about the therapeutic relationship.

Sándor Ferenczi and Sigmund Freud, here at a meeting in 1917, developed different ideas about therapists' approach to their patients.

He criticized Freud for shaping his relationship toward patients into a "medical-therapeutic procedure." (Psychoanalysis had indeed developed out of hypnosis.) Now that Freud had abandoned hypnosis, Fromm considered that he did not give sufficient thought to the "modern, humane side of the situation." "The analyst should maintain 'evenly suspended attention,' and should become 'neutral' and 'emotionally cold', he should be free of 'therapeutic ambition' and under no circumstances give in to the patient's desire for love. He should be 'opaque' to the patient, smooth as a mirror's surface."[52]

Fromm had learned Freud's classical psychoanalytic technique in his own training analysis with Hanns Sachs in Berlin and had practiced it for some time. He thus criticized Freud's rules both on the basis of his own therapeutic experiences and as a result of his own theoretical approach. He justified his criticism in a letter to Otto Fenichel dated the 19th of March, 1936, writing "during the last few years I have come increasingly to the conclusion that the comparable attitudes toward the patient of Freud, Sachs, and others not only reduce the effect of the therapy, but can also do serious harm to some patients."

Taking Groddeck (above) and Ferenczi (below) as an example, Fromm explains what he means by the "humane side" of the therapeutic relationship: "[Groddeck's] attitude toward patients was not soft, but full of humanity and real friendliness. For him the patient was at the center, and the analyst had to serve him. His effectiveness was mostly a personal one and the development of Ferenczi is to be understood through the strong influence of Groddeck."[52]

Fromm's new psychoanalytic approach made this criticism necessary. According to Fromm, psychological structures and neurotic conflicts result from one's actual experience of connecting with outer and inner realities. The inner reality comprises internalized representations of objects and the self, images that usually form during the first few years of life. So Fromm rejects Freud's idea that psychological structures develop through an automatic process whereby one or several built-in drives or partial drives experience and come to terms with reality.

Because of this fundamentally different psychoanalytic approach, the "humane side" of the therapeutic relationship deserves far more attention, according to Fromm: "Ferenczi was full of productive fantasy and warm, though at the same time, in contrast to Groddeck, soft and anxious. As positive features of an analyst he demanded tact and kindness. He mentions as an example the ability to recognize 'when the silence (of the analyst) causes unnecessary torment to the patient.' He did not force the patient during the analysis to lie down and have the analyst invisible behind him. He analyzed also in cases were the patient was unable to pay. He often prolonged a session to avoid the shock of a sudden interruption. He also analyzed patients if necessary for two or more hours on the same day."[52]

In this essay from 1935 Fromm already saw that Ferenczi was in fundamental contradiction with Freud over his manner of relating to patients. It is "the difference between a humane, kind attitude which wholeheartedly promotes the well-being of the patient, in contrast to a patricentric-authoritarian, basically misanthropic 'tolerance.'"[52]

It should be pointed out that Ferenczi did not see erotic love as a model for the therapeutic relationship; the analyst was to feel "no erotic love but rather motherly or fatherly love or, putting it more generally, loving care."[53]

Much of what Fromm here said about Ferenczi, he himself held to be true and practiced.[54] To distinguish his own therapeutic approach, he later referred back to Ferenczi and Sullivan.

"Sullivan thought that the analyst must not have the attitude of a detached observer, but of a 'participant observer.' In my own view, Sullivan may not have gone far enough, and one might prefer the definition of the analyst's role as that of an 'observant participant.'"

"But even the expression 'participant' does not quite express what is meant here; to participate is still to be outside.

The knowledge of another person requires being inside him, to be him. The analyst understands the patient only inasmuch as he experiences in himself all that the patient experiences. In this productive relatedness between analyst and patient, in the act of being

George Groddeck's and Sándor Ferenczi's "humane" attitude toward therapeutic practise shaped the understanding of Erich Fromm, Frieda Fromm-Reichmann, and Karen Horney. The cooperation of these three with Harry Stack Sullivan (picture) led to the theory and practice of "Interpersonal Psychoanalysis", which incorporated many of the insights of Ferenczi and Groddeck who died in 1933 and 1934. These insights survived and blossomed anew in the works of Harry Stack Sullivan, Frieda Fromm-Reichmann, and Clara Thompson.

fully engaged with the patient, in being fully open and responsive to him, in being soaked in him, as it were, in this *center-to-center relatedness* lies one of the essential conditions for psychoanalytic understanding and cure."

"The analyst must become the patient, yet he must be himself; he must forget, that he is the doctor, yet he must remain aware of it. Only when he accepts this paradox, can he give 'interpretations' that carry authority because they are rooted in his own experience.

Frieda Fromm-Reichmann (picture) and Erich Fromm lived apart from 1931 and were divorced at the beginning of the 'forties. Nevertheless, they shared the same therapeutic convictions and remained friends until her death in 1957.

The analyst analyzes the patient, but the patient also analyzes the analyst, because the analyst, by sharing the unconscious of his patient, cannot help clarifying his own unconscious. Hence the analyst not only cures the patient, but is also cured by him."[53]

There is no doubt Fromm's understanding of the role of the therapist considers the "modern, humane side of the situation"[52] within the therapeutic process in a totally different way from Freud. Ferenczi and Sullivan were the midwives for Fromm's own therapeutic approach as well a for his therapeutic identity. At the Washington School of Psychiatry, Sullivan offered Fromm a new psychoanalytic spiritual home in several respects.

With the help of the William Alanson White Psychiatric Foundation, from 1938 on, Sullivan was able to publish the psychiatric magazine *Psychiatry: Journal for the Study of Interpersonal Process*, to which Fromm contributed four important articles between 1939 and 1943.

The Institute for Social Research refused to publish his "Fundamental Essay" written in 1937 for the *Zeitschrift für Sozialforschung* (*Studies in Philosophies and Social Sciences*). Later, *Psychiatry*, the publication of the Washington School of Psychiatry became the place were his thoughts were welcomed.

Sullivan's Washington School of Psychiatry, founded in 1936, became Fromm's new home in another respect. He now could pass on his new psychoanalytic approach to practicing therapists at this institute. He also came into contact with potential patients.

For Fromm, as for all psychoanalytic immigrants, it was difficult to find patients. Until 1936 he mainly analyzed sociologists and anthropologists—those who wanted to apply psychoanalysis within their fields.

With his psychoanalytic teachings, his interests shifted: he now was much more in demand as a theoretician of psychoanalysis and as a psychoanalytic clinician not so much as an empirical social-psychologist and member of the Institute for Social Research.

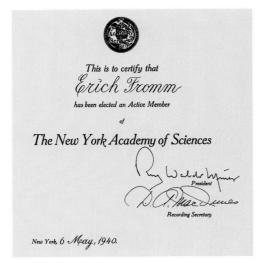

This is to certify that

Erich Fromm

has been elected an Active Member

of

The New York Academy of Sciences

President

Recording Secretary

New York, 6 May, 1940.

After separation from the Institute for Social Research, Fromm sought more direct contact with American scientists and institutes. In 1940, he was elected a member of the New York Academy of Science.

Like Sullivan, Karen Horney provided Fromm with a new professional home. In 1941, together with members of the Washington School of Psychiatry in New York, she founded the Association for the Advancement of Psychoanalysis. There Erich Fromm was temporarily given the right to conduct clinical seminars. In 1943, however, the long and fruitful friendship came to an end.

It is not by chance that Fromm published his essays in Sullivan's *Psychiatry* for the first time in English. Now that he had found a new spiritual home as a psychoanalyst, he wrote in English. The "Fundamental Essay" of 1937, which perhaps marked the transition from his old home in the Institute for Social Research and the new in the Washington School of Psychiatry, had been written in German.[55] The change of language points to his new identity as a psychoanalyst with a new approach in theory and practice and also to his American identity (although he did not become a citizen until 1940).

His first chance to make an active contribution to the clinical training of psychoanalysts came in 1941, when Karen Horney and others left the New York Psychoanalytic Society following a dispute.[56] Karen Horney was, as a medically qualified doctor, a member of this psychoanalytic society and active within therapeutic training. This right was disputed after she published her book *The Neurotic Personality of Our Time* and resulted in the foundation of a new society, the Association for the Advancement of Psychoanalysis (AAP).

Erich Fromm, a member of the group since its formation, was to become an honorary member, since he had no medical qualification. He was opposed to this, however, and made his membership dependent on his being fully recognized as a training analyst with supervisory responsibility. This happened in November 1941.

Conflict about Fromm's status was predictable, however. A year later, in January 1943, students applied to the faculty-board for permission for Fromm to hold

Clara Thompson became an important advocate for Erich Fromm's professional recognition in the U.S.A. She took Sullivan's advice and traveled several times each year to Sándor Ferenczi in Budapest where she would stay for some weeks. In 1930, she became the first president of the newly founded Washington-Baltimore Psychoanalytic Society. From 1933, she lived in New York and continued her didactic analysis with Erich Fromm from 1934 onwards. She was at his side during the many disputes in psychoanalytic circles and at the foundation of each new grouping. She was cofounder of the William Alanson White Institute in New York and remained the leading light there until her death in December 1958.

a "technical" seminar "in light of his stimulating clinical presentation."[47]

The board of Karen Horney's institute rejected the application because psychoanalysis by medically unqualified personnel would then be officially sanctioned. A suggestion for a compromise, which was to confine Fromm to theoretical groups excluding clinical seminars, was rejected. Clara Thompson, president of the institute at that time, declared her solidarity with Fromm and left along with others in April 1943.

Biographers of Karen Horney give other reasons for the change in the professional relationship between Horney and Fromm. Their personal relations became more intimate in 1934, just as Fromm's influence and fame as a psychoanalyst grew. This must have been difficult for her.

With his book *Escape from Freedom* in 1941, Fromm became suddenly famous. "There is much testimony that Horney envied Fromm's new fame and his success as a teacher and wanted 'to be the one and only star' at the institute."[57]

In addition both had close relationships with others: Karen Horney with Paul Tillich and Erich Maria Remarque; Erich Fromm with the twenty-nine-year-old dancer, choreographer, and ballet mistress, Katherine Dunham. Fromm's behavior hurt Horney so deeply that she split up not only with him, but also with Ernst Schachtel, because he continued to see Fromm.

"Horney never found another lover of the stature of Erich Fromm, nor did she expose herself again to the kind of disappointment she had experienced with him. She rushed from one relationship into another, but she protected herself by not investing her feelings as deeply as she had done with Fromm."[57]

The William Alanson White Institute (WAWI) at 20, West 74th Street in New York. Erich Fromm helped found the institute in 1943 and stayed in touch throughout his life, even after his move to Mexico. He held seminars and worked as a training analyst and supervisor.

Some of those who had left Horney's Association for the Advancement of Psychoanalysis (AAP) in 1943 joined members of the Washington-Baltimore Psychoanalytic Society to set up a New York branch of the Washington School of Psychiatry.

The founders were Harry Stack Sullivan, Erich Fromm, Frieda Fromm-Reichmann, Clara Thompson, David and Janet Rioch. A little later, Ralph Crowley, Hilde Bruch, and Meyer Maskin joined in. To get things off the ground, Sullivan, Frieda Fromm-Reichmann and David Rioch traveled every three weeks from Washington to New York.

After World War II, activities could be significantly expanded. In 1946, the New York branch was renamed the William Alanson White Institute of Psychiatry, Psychoanalysis, and Psychology. As in the Washington School, the study of psychoanalysis was linked to other human and social sciences.

Fromm's aims were "[to] train psychiatrists and psychologists in the theory and practice of psychoanalysis, and to instruct teachers, ministers, social workers, nurses, and physicians in the psychoanalytic concepts which will extend their skills in their own professions."[58]

As a further special feature at one of the first clinics, the institute ran an autclinic, which was available also for people in reduced circumstances. In 1946, Fromm took charge of the training and the supervision of the teachers. In June 1950, he moved to Mexico. From 1953 onwards, he returned every year, however, for several months to lecture and hold clinical seminars at the institute in New York.

On his difficult journey to a psychoanalytic identity and a spiritual home, Fromm concerned himself for several years with the psychodynamics of authoritarian structures.

In a section on social psychology in his *Studien über Autorität und Familie* (*Studies in Authority and Family*), 1936, he explained the authoritarian character with reference to sadomasochism:

Sozialpsychologischer Teil.
Von
Erich Fromm.

Inhalt. I. *Einleitung. Mannigfaltigkeit der Autoritätserscheinungen.* S. 77. — II. *Autorität und Über-Ich. Die Rolle der Familie bei ihrer Entwicklung.* S. 80. — III. *Autorität und Verdrängung.* S. 93. — IV. *Der autoritär-masochistische Charakter.* S. 110.

I. Einleitung.
Mannigfaltigkeit der Autoritätserscheinungen.

Bei vielen Menschen ist ihr Verhältnis zur Autorität der hervorstechendste Zug ihres Charakters : sei es, dass die einen nur dann eigentlich glücklich sind, wenn sie sich einer Autorität fügen und unterwerfen können, und um so mehr, je strenger und rücksichtsloser diese ist, sei es, dass andere sich auflehnend und trotzig verhalten, sowie sie auch nur irgendwo sich Anordnungen fügen sollen, und wären es auch die vernünftigsten und für sie selbst zweckmässigsten. Während aber andere Charakterzüge wie etwa Geiz oder Pünktlichkeit eine relativ einheitliche Erscheinung darstellen, ist das Bild, das uns die Aufzählung auch nur weniger Beispiele von verschiedenen Arten der Autorität und der Einstel-

Fromm's most important publication at the Institute for Social Research was *Studien über Autorität und Familie* (Studies in Authority and Family) in 1936. In the section on social psychology, Fromm developed the concept of the authoritarian character. His idea of explaining the authoritarian character through the psychodynamics of sadomasochism, led to a debate about authoritarianism which found its climax in the discussion about antiauthoritarian education in the 'sixties.

"A person with masochistic tendencies seeks to abandon his individuality to another authority sacrificing his own happiness. The aim is to dissolve in [another's power] and to find pleasure and satisfaction within this surrender. In pathological cases this involves incurring physical pain. In opposition, one with sadistic tendencies seeks to destroy the will of another, make him a defenseless and will-less instrument of his own will, to dominate him absolutely, in extreme cases forcing him to suffer and to express the feelings induced by this suffering."[59]

It seemed natural to use this notion of the authoritarian character to explain the rise of fascism in Germany and Italy. As early as 1936, Fromm started to write a book, which he intended to call *Der Mensch im autoritären Staat* (*The Individual in the Authoritarian State*). In 1941 it became his first best-seller, *Escape from Freedom.* In it he analyzed the authoritarian character and the psychology of Nazism, but expanded his perspective to incorporate the notion of escape into authoritarianism within a history of freedom in the modern age.

With the publication of this book in 1941, Fromm suddenly found himself in the academic and political limelight. With the help of his theory of the authoritarian character, Fromm could explain specifically why the petty bourgeoisie in Germany and Italy, driven into insignificance, sought salvation by submitting to a megalomaniac leader–Führer or Duce–following him in blind obedience.

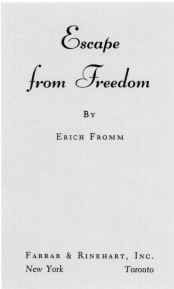

Escape

from Freedom

By

Erich Fromm

Farrar & Rinehart, Inc.
New York   Toronto

With the publication of *Escape from Freedom* in 1941, Fromm suddenly became known to the American public as a psychoanalyst of society.

There was no particular submissive instinct; neither was the German national character particularly destructive. It was rather the desperate economic and social circumstances of the petty bourgeoisie after World War I, brought about by staggering inflation and a worldwide depression, that lay behind this escape into authoritarianism. This reaction brought Hitler to power and led most Germans blindly to follow his destructive exercise of force.

Six years after his emigration, Fromm became an American citizen on the 25th of May, 1940. Meanwhile, his political thinking became more American. The disputes with the Institute for Social Research were confined to the past just as much as his tuberculosis. His own understanding of psychoanalysis in theory and clinical practice was defined and was enthusiastically discussed in the Sullivan circle. With this first major book, his psychoanalytic theory passed its first crucial test.

The war raging in Europe did not prevent Fromm from making use of his newly found identity and freedom. After his relationship with Karen Horney ended in 1943, and, while he was friends with Katherine Dunham, he had an affair with Martha Graham, also a dancer, choreographer, and ballet director.

During this period he met Henny Gurland, at the home of the photographer, Ruth Staudinger, daughter of the president of the New School of Social Research.

Gurland had fled the Nazis from France together with her seventeen-year-old son Joseph and had come to New York in December 1940. On the 24th of July, 1944, Fromm and she were married.

Who was Henny Gurland-Fromm? She was born on the 27th of September, 1900 as the second child of Augusta and Leopold Meyer in Aachen. As the daughter of a Jewish father and a Catholic mother she was educated by Catholic nuns. Instead of studying after her final school exams, she was trained as a secretary and found work in Berlin. There she also met her first husband, Otto Rosenthal, whom she married in 1922 in Frankfurt am Main. Joseph was born in 1923. But the marriage was not to last. During divorce procedures in 1929, his father obtained custody.

On the 24th of July, 1944, Fromm married in New York for the second time. His new wife, Henny Gurland-Fromm, was born in 1900 in Aachen, Germany, and fled in September 1940 from Nazi-occupied France.

➤

During her escape from the Nazis, Henny witnessed Walter Benjamin's suicide at the Spanish border town of Port-Bou on the 25th of September, 1940.

This picture is misleading: Fromm's relationship with his twenty-one-year-old stepson Joseph, far from being strict or authoritarian, was friendly.

Henny Gurland was politically engaged with the Social Democrats and, at the time Hitler came to power in January 1933, worked as a photographer for the social democratic newspaper *Vorwärts*. After the Nazis searched her house, she fled to Brussels. In 1934 she secretly took her son, known as Josi, from Germany. In 1936, she married Rafael Gurland, a diplomat acting for the Spanish Republic, at that time stationed in Brussels and later in Paris.

She went to Paris with her husband, but they drifted apart. At the beginning of the war in 1939, he fought on the side of the French and became a German prisoner of war in May 1940. As the Germans advanced on Paris, Henny Gurland left and arranged a United States visa for herself and her son. They lacked exit visas from France, however. So, along with Walter Benjamin, she attempted an illegal crossing of the unguarded border to Spain in September 1940. They were caught by Spanish border guards who proposed to return them to France.

In these desperate circumstances, Walter Benjamin, who was Jewish, and had good reason to fear the Nazi-controlled French administration, committed suicide before Henny's eyes. Showing great presence of mind, she managed to conceal the act, however, passing off his death as heart failure and then took care of his burial.

In order to avoid trouble over Benjamin's death, the border guards allowed Henny Gurland to travel on with her son. In Lisbon, the two waited for three months for a place on a ship. It was the *Siboney* that eventually brought them to New York.

Her marriage to Rafael Gurland, who operated under the alias "Thomas," was dissolved in 1943. This left her free to marry Erich Fromm, her third husband, in July 1944. In the middle of the 'forties they moved into a new flat at 322 Central Park West in New York. They did not have children together, but Erich Fromm looked after his twenty-one-year-old stepson like a father.

In a letter Henny Fromm wrote on 6th May 1946 to Izette de Forest she writes: "Erich likes family life very much, His attitude toward Josi is wonderful—he is like a friend and father."

About her love to Erich she writes in the same letter: "His harmonious way of dealing with difficulties makes me love him even more than I did before—but you know Erich and his good influence, and I don't have to tell you how happy I am with him."

Henny Fromm introduced her husband to Charlotte Selver, the grande dame of the then fashionable Sensory Awareness movement. Selver recalled in 1997 (at the age of ninety-seven) the day

in 1942 when she first met the psychoanalyst. There followed a period when she went to Central Park West every morning to instruct Fromm in body awareness exercises while his wife was baking rolls for breakfast.[39]

She also remembers that he was a man with little time. He was an interested lecturer, scientist, and therapist, engaged in various professional and political circles, always busy and driven. His conclusions were blunt and penetrating, so much so that some criticized him for being arrogant and impatient. His output of essays and books in the 'forties was, however, less prolific than at other phases of his life. He paid more attention at this time to psychoanalytic training, including university lecturing, in Washington and New York.

Whenever his agenda allowed, Fromm spent his weekends with his wife, Henny, in Bennington, Vermont, where, from 1942 onwards, he held a part-time professorship.

During the 'forties, Fromm divided his week between the city and a country town. From midday Tuesday until noon on Friday, he lived in New York working with patients or lecturing at the New School for Social Research. From Friday evening until Tuesday morning, he stayed in Irish Corners, North Bennington, enjoying the fresh air and walking his dog, Bingo. On Mondays he taught at Bennington College.

Between 1941 and 1949, apart from his work with patients and aspiring psychoanalysts, Fromm became a lecturer at the New School for Social Research in New York and a professor at the Bennington College in Vermont. It was a particular honor for him to be invited to lecture at Yale University on religion during the winter semester 1948-49. In these lectures, which he published under the title *Psychoanalysis and Religion* in 1950, Fromm first distinguished his own religious critique from those of Freud and Jung.

The themes of the seminars and lectures at the New School were mostly the relationship between society and psychological structures; culture and personality. He also introduced his students to psychoanalysis and the interpretation of dreams. In spring 1942, eight of his fifteen lectures discussed "Society and Psychoanalysis." He developed his concept of individual and social character, explaining the impact of economic, social, and political factors on the psychic structure of the individual. Repeatedly he offered lectures on the significance of "emotional forces in the social process." Most of the chapters of his second book, *Man for Himself* (1947), are to be found in the list of lectures at the New School from the 'forties.

Even after he moved to Mexico, Fromm came to the New School in New York each spring until 1959. Here, in 1953, he developed his ideas on the alienation of the marketing oriented society and on "The Pathology of Normalcy," which play a major role in his book *The Sane Society* (1955).

His other university duties during the 'forties were in Bennington, a small college town in the state of Vermont, about 250 kilometers (150 miles) north of New York. Here he dealt mainly with questions of ethics in the tradition of Aristotle and Spinoza, but also with the connection between human nature and character structure and with the symbolic language of the unconscious. These themes can also be found in his books *Man for Himself* (1947) and *The Forgotten Language* (1951).

Fromm was very much liked by the students at the all-female Bennington College, as this obituary in the *Bennington Quadrille* for 1980 illustrates: "He was known for his custom of teaching on Mondays, leaving town on Tuesdays to practice psychoanalysis in various cities, then returning from New York on Fridays with a satchel full of gourmet edibles he had bought in delicatessens; he would then invite friends to his home on the Murphy Road to partake of the food."

Bennington was very attractive, so in 1946, Erich and Henny decided to build a seven-room house at 228 Murphy Road. They moved in toward the end of the summer of 1948. As they were moving, Henny became ill with arthritis and was confined to bed for long periods because of the pain.

With an annual endowment of $2500, the professorship in Bennington offered Henny and Erich Fromm the chance to escape New York over the weekends. Little wonder that they started to build a house in Bennington in 1946. In late summer of 1948 they were able to move from the rented accommodation at Irish Corners in North Bennington to the new house in Murphy Road.

The move into the new house was overshadowed by Henny Fromm's illness. She suffered increasingly from arthritic pain, which became unbearable. She needed Fromm's whole attention and he had to cancel almost all of his invitations for lectures in 1948 and 1949. On the 3rd of June, 1949, he wrote to the wife of Henny's brother Arno (Arnold): "Henny has been rather ill, sometimes with severe pain, so she has not been able to sleep for many nights. For three-quarters of a year she

has almost always been in bed unable to do anything, not even write letters. I have not been able to write. Apart from my practice and other professional duties, I have been busy with Henny's illness."

First it was thought, that lead poisoning was causing Henny's sickness, or perhaps that injuries she had endured during her escape from Paris could be responsible for the pain. Apparently medicine was unable to cure her mysterious illness.

Finally doctors recommended a stay in Mexico. So in summer 1949, they traveled for a few week to the radioactive springs in San José Purua. The climate soothed the pain somewhat.

On the 6th of June, 1950, they moved to Mexico City so Henny would be able to spend more time in San José Purua. Henny's illness remained mysterious, however, and her health failed to improve to any great

extent. She died on the 4th of June, 1952. Fromm's decision to move to Mexico had been primarily out of love for Henny.

6
The Art of Loving
and the Reality of the
Destructive Urge

Fromm lived from 1950 until 1973 in Mexico.

"His eyes could also become severe and during his first years with us, they could appear haughty, a haughtiness also apparent in his bearing. His self-analysis, his increasing capacity to love, his joy of living, and his creative life produced a visible change and he became a kindly, amiable, simple man—that haughty vanity of his first years disappeared never to return."[60]

Jorge Silva, who wrote these words, belonged to the first generation of psychoanalysts whom Fromm trained between 1951 and 1956 in Mexico. Fromm moved to Mexico mainly because of his wife Henny's illness but also because he was interested in educating Mexican psychoanalysts: psychoanalysis was hardly known in Mexico at that time.

It was mainly due to Henny's illness that Fromm was bound so strongly to Mexico. He could not leave her alone for very long and she was not able to travel far. In fact, after his emigration to Mexico, Fromm spent the first two years—until Henny's death—exclusively in that country. He was unable to fulfill his educational commitments in Bennington, at the New School for Social Research, nor at the White Institute in New York.

Fromm made new professional contacts at first through the children's psychiatrist José F. Diaz and the director of the Universidad National Autónoma de Mexico (UNAM), Jesos Zozaya.

In 1950, they persuaded Fromm to give a seminar in the auditorium of the Puebla Street Hospital at the corner of Orizaba Street in Mexico City. Aimed at psychiatrists, it dealt with the symbolic language of the unconscious.

From these beginnings, a plan developed for a five-year course in psychoanalysis for psychiatrists. The course began in 1951 and was usually held in Fromm's apartment in Guttenberg Street, then later at 71 Anatole France Street in Mexico City. He took up a professorship at the university, which he held until his retirement in 1965.

Although Fromm used his own psychoanalytic approach in theory and therapeutic practice, the main theoretical basis for the education of the Mexican psychoanalysts was the writing of Freud.

The work of Ferenczi, Sullivan, Horney, and Fromm-Reichmann extended the scope of the course. With regard to the therapeutic work, Fromm focused entirely on the "humane side" of the therapeutic relationship.

From time to time, lecturers from New York were invited to supervise and lecture. This way, the Mexican students came to know Michael Balint, Clara Thompson, John Thompson, Nathan Ackerman, Edward S. Tauber, Rose Spiegel, Ben Weininger, David Schecter, Roy R. Grinker, Paul Tillich, Judd Marmor, Sir Stephen Kinghall, Daisetz T. Suzuki, and Charlotte Selver.

Erich Fromm with Jorge Silva, a psychoanalyst from the first generation that Fromm educated. Lectures and clinical seminars were generally held by Fromm. Also, all thirteen participants of the first course[60] had their training analysis with him (two hours each week).

Alfonso Millán (center) was the first president of the Sociedad Psicoanalítica Mexicana, which was founded in 1956. Aniceto Aramoni (right) later became the director of the institute and made his mark through numerous publications.

In 1956, after finishing the first course, the group founded its own psychoanalytic society, called *Sociedad Psicoanalítica Mexicana* and in 1963 the society moved into its own institute, in a building close to the university. This was possible largely thanks to the efforts of Jorge Silva who planned the building and came up with ideas for financing.

Regarding psychoanalytic training Fromm "insisted, again and again, that psychoanalysis must be, from the very beginning, a non-alienated relationship, precisely because its goal is to derepress and disalienate. Thus it must be a meaningful dialogue—vis à vis—during which neither subject of the dyad can hide from the other. While facing one another we convey both our verbal and, most significantly, our non-verbal communications."[61]

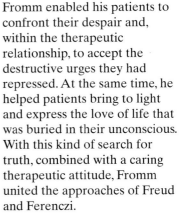

With great self-discipline, Fromm meditated every day and analyzed his dreams.

The Instituto Mexicano de Psicoanálisis at 9, Calle de Odontologia in Mexico City was opened on the 8th of March, 1963. The building, planned by Jorge Silva, has a psychotherapeutic outclinic, counseling rooms, a library, seminar rooms, and an auditorium for public lectures. In the second floor, an apartment was provided in which Erich Fromm or guests of the institute could stay.

Fromm enabled his patients to confront their despair and, within the therapeutic relationship, to accept the destructive urges they had repressed. At the same time, he helped patients bring to light and express the love of life that was buried in their unconscious. With this kind of search for truth, combined with a caring therapeutic attitude, Fromm united the approaches of Freud and Ferenczi.

At the same time, he distanced himself ever more from the attempt by "official" psychoanalysis to turn the therapeutic relationship—dealing with the patient—into a learnable "technique." The therapist should first of all learn to recognize his own destructive and creative impulses. Fromm believed that training analysis and regular, lifelong self-analysis were the most important aids to understanding.

The more a person can relate to his own hidden forces, the more loving and giving he can be to other people and the less the danger that therapy will decay into conversation. With the passing of time, Fromm increasingly saw the unconscious as a creative wellspring of humanity. The unconscious is not only that which is repressed because it is unacceptable to society, but the whole human being with all his deep and imaginative potential.

Fromm's understanding of the unconscious as a representation of the entire individual was furthered by his study of Zen Buddhism. He first came across Daisetz T. Suzuki, the

Fromm's enduring bonds with the New York based Zen Buddhist, Daisetz T. Suzuki led to a seminar in Mexico in 1957 during which Fromm attempted to define a therapeutic approach to the unconscious, derived from the principles of Zen. Fromm's contribution was published in 1960 under the title *Psychoanalysis and Zen Buddhism* and is without a doubt the best of Fromm's writing on the unconscious and psychoanalysis.

great promoter of Zen Buddhism, in the 'forties. But it was only after Suzuki visited him in late 1956 in Mexico, and Fromm returned the visit in New York, that the psychoanalyst first had "the feeling that I understood Zen, as if something had 'clicked,' as they say."[134]

In August 1957, a one-week seminar with the eighty-six-year-old Suzuki was held in Mexico. All attention was directed toward the modest Zen Buddhist, but perhaps the most important contribution came from Fromm. In his paper, "Psychoanalysis and Zen-Buddhism", he showed how the principles of Zen may be applied to psychoanalysis.

Fromm was especially interested in the experience of oneness with the object of perception. This idea, so important in Zen, was imaginatively embodied and

demonstrated by Suzuki who would use, for example, a rose or a cat to invoke this state. (Suzuki actually went missing during one of his stays with Fromm, while, for three hours, he did nothing but watch one of Fromm's wife's cats.)

Zen Buddhism and psychoanalysis both offer ways of experiencing oneness of the outer and inner realities, in which the limits of the Ego are overcome and the human can become united with the unconscious, unbound by time or space. This can occur without psychotic disintegration of the Ego.

Standing beside Daisetz T. Suzuki are Erich and Annis Fromm: in front of Suzuki his secretary Okamura; far right Aniceto Aramoni.

Among the forty or so American and Mexican psychoanalysts were Jorge Silva (left) and Francisco Garza. Frieda Fromm-Reichmann, who had also wanted to attend, died in 1957 at Chestnut Lodge.

Throughout his life, Fromm was searching for this experience of oneness, which is the main aim of Zen Buddhism. He meditated every day and analyzed his dreams.

"I read every morning either some Zen text or Meister Eckhart," he wrote on the 29th of April, 1964, to the ninety-three-year-old Suzuki, who was now back in Japan.

Fromm read widely in the mystical traditions of various religions. He discovered this experience of oneness in the Cabala and in Hasidism, in the Christian mystics such as Meister Eckhart and Jakob Böhme, in Islam with the Sufism of Rumi, in Zen Buddhism as taught by Suzuki, and in the Buddhism that Nyanaponika Mahathera expounded toward the end of his life.

Fromm felt the experience of oneness also in the philosophical idea of the One in the writings of Plotinus and Pseudo-Dionysus Areopagita as well as in the Judeo-Christian tradition. His lasting interest in religion was directed toward the experience of the One or, as he writes in his book, *You Shall Be as Gods*, of the "X-experience," which cannot be named. According to Fromm, this concept of the "unnamable" contradicts the dogmatic assertions of established religions. For this reason, he remained throughout his life a sharp critic of all institutionalized religion.

In secular form, Fromm saw the experience of oneness flowering within Renaissance humanism in the idea of the universal human.

"The most fundamental idea of humanism is the idea that all of humanity is contained in each man, and that man develops his humanity in the historical process."[63]

Zen Buddhism brought Fromm to the realization that the unconscious represents the universal in the individual human: "The unconscious is the whole man—minus that part of man which corresponds to his society."[63]

So Fromm concluded that the realization of oneness first becomes known in the experience of making the unconscious conscious and that a psycho-analysis, which aims to reveal the unconscious, is thus able to reestablish humanism: "Making the unconscious conscious transforms the mere idea of the universality of man into the living experience of this universality; it is the experiential realization of humanity."[63]

With this understanding of humanistic psycho-analysis (which has little in common with what is nowadays labeled "humanistic psychology") Fromm sought more contact with other psychoanalytic associations outside the orthodox International Psychoanalytic Association (IPA) and that did not

At an international congress organized by the German Psychoanalytic Society in Düsseldorf in September 1961 Fromm lectured on the "Basic Position of Psychoanalysis" in which he attempted to summarize the common denominator of the nonorthodox psychoanalytic societies. In the first row are Annelise Heigl-Evers and her husband Franz Heigl, who played a major role in realizing the International Federation of Psychoanalytic Societies (IFPS). Today twenty-two associations belong to the Federation.[56]

The Düsseldorf congress of 1961 reestablished Fromm's contact with many European psychoanalysts, for example Fritz Riemann (right), with whom Fromm was connected until the seventies.

want to become members because of the IPA's predominant dogmatism.

Toward the end of June 1961 Fromm met with Werner Schwidder and Franz Heigl from the German Psychoanalytic Society in Paris to make plans for a merger of nonorthodox groups. In 1962 the International Federation of Psychoanalytic Societies (IFPS) was founded in Amsterdam. It included the German Psychoanalytic Society, Fromm's Mexican Group, the Austrian group around Igor Caruso, and the William Alanson White Institute in New York, represented by Gerard Chrzanowski.

On the 18th of December,
1953, Erich Fromm
married Annis Freeman,
née Glover. Erich Fromm's
mother was also present.

In 1952, Annis Freeman
lost her husband David
with whom she had lived
for several years in India.

Immediately after his move to Mexico, Fromm's private life was determined totally by Henny's illness. Her death on the 4th of June, 1952, brought on a feeling of total helplessness—all his love and care had been unable to save her.

Only slowly did the pain recede. Eventually, Fromm took up the threads of his life again and made new contacts. One of these was Annis Freeman from Philadelphia, whose husband David–a lawyer and newspaper publisher in India–had recently died.

Fromm got to know him and his wife at the end of 1948 in New York in connection with a UNESCO project on political tensions. (This project had envisaged Fromm's doing field research in Australia, but he had to give up these plans because of Henny's illness.)

His renewed contact with Annis blossomed into an intense and tender love that lasted twenty-eight years until Fromm's death.

In contrast to Karen Horney, this tall, self-assured, intelligent, attractive, and sensuous women knew nothing of ambition and rivalry.

Once, it seems, Fromm introduced her jokingly as "the laziest person in the world."

But Freeman was by no means lazy; like Fromm, she was interested in international politics, the diversity of cultures and the manifold forms of social organization. During her stay in India she became acquainted with Indian culture and the Eastern spiritual tradition.

Fromm always saw her as an equal partner in scientific discussions; she read all his manuscripts and made critical comments. She also, however, displayed a lively interest in palmistry and astrology.

Fromm fell in love with Annis and courted her like a medieval minstrel–not with songs, but in his whole manner, with loving and tender words, pictures, glances, feelings, and gestures. His ability to love was extraordinary. He experienced a physical need for her that had to express itself. The intensity of his love never waned even after twenty-five years of marriage.

Annis was two years younger than her husband and an American through and through. Though born in Pittsburgh, she grew up in Alabama and spoke with a distinctly Southern accent, which the naturalized Erich Fromm found occasionally challenging.

When, for example, they took the three-person elevator to their fifth-floor apartment in the Casa La Monda in Locarno, Muralto, although he was seventy-eight and she seventy-six, they still felt compelled to gaze into each other's eyes and exchange a kiss. The need to feel and express their love lasted until they died.

Fromm practiced loving like a sensual talent. Just as most people perceive the world with their eyes, he had the ability to perceive and connect to other people lovingly, so loving became an indispensable part of his approach to life.

Fromm's need to love manifested itself not only in his erotic desire for Annis, but also in the way he dealt with other people. Annis collected hundreds of pieces of paper with little messages (like the one printed above) which he had written to her over a few years.

At the end of 1953, Annis Freeman and Erich Fromm were married. Doubtless the experience of their love made its mark on *The Art of Loving*, which Fromm published shortly afterwards. Otherwise, perhaps the book would not have met with such lasting success. What Fromm writes here about the ability to love derives directly from his own knowledge and practice.

To be able to love is not a question of being loved or being in love, rather the realization of potential inherent within each individual: being able to connect lovingly with the inner and outer realities. Love is a "power of its own," which becomes potent insofar as it is practiced. To the same extent, it also develops into a need to love; the individual lives from his or her center, strength, and being.

"Love is possible only if two persons communicate with each other from the center of their existence, and if each one of them experiences himself from the center of his existence. Only in this "central experience" is human reality, only here is aliveness, only here is the basis for love. Love, experienced thus, is a constant challenge; it is not a resting place, but a moving, growing, working together; even whether there is harmony or conflict, joy or sadness, is secondary to the fundamental fact that two people experience themselves from the essence of their existence, that they are one with each other by being one with themselves, rather than by fleeing from themselves". [64]

Shortly after their marriage at the end of 1953, they planned to build a house in Mexico. As he had in New York, Fromm wanted to keep a small flat in Mexico City (at 15 Gonzales Cosio Street), but the main residence was to be in Cuernavaca, 9,200 feet above sea level and forty three miles from Mexico City. Annis, who was quite wealthy after her marriage with David Freeman, supervised the plans for the new house, which was to accommodate Fromm's practice and a seminar room. They moved in at the end of 1956 and in time made acquaintances in the neighborhood.

Ivan Illich, who became known for his social criticism of educational systems and medical practice, had abandoned his career as a Roman Catholic church diplomat to set up an information center in Cuernavaca for the emancipation of politically-oppressed Latin Americans. It was known as the Centro Intercultural de Documentación (CIDOC). Through this center Fromm met Paulo Freire, the educationalist who campaigned for the goal of universal literacy in Latin America. He also maintained contact with Father Wasson and considered the educational principles that Wasson put into effect at his neighborhood orphanage that eventually took care of 1,200 children.

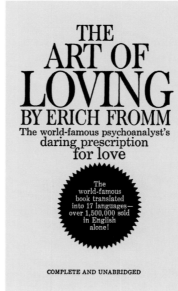

In 1956 this little book about the art of loving was first published. Since then, it has been translated into fifty languages and has sold 25 million copies.

Below: The mountain slope to the pass at 9 Neptuno Street, where Erich and Annis Fromm bought a large plot. Here they built their new home. A brook ran through their land, which had a parklike garden.

The select resort of Cuernavaca is separated from Mexico City by a pass–3500 meters (11,500 feet) above sea level at its highest point. The climate is much better here than in Mexico City.

The house in Cuernavaca, planned by Annis Fromm, also housed Fromm's psychotherapeutic practice.

For ten years, from the end of the 'fifties, Fromm researched the social character of some

800 Mexican farmers in Chiconcuac.

Almost every week, Fromm went to Mexico City in his big Buick for two days to work at the psychoanalytic institute in the medical faculty at the University of Mexico. At that time, it was still located in Liverpool Street He started to lecture in Spanish and became interested in the sociopolitical problems of Mexico. Under President Alfonso Lopez Mateos (1958-64), he developed, in cooperation with Hank Gonzalez, director of the Almacenes Generales de Deposito, a system that was supposed to secure for farmers a fair price for their produce.

Fromm became more and more interested in the life of his adopted land, Mexico: a third-world country with a rich cultural heritage and outstanding natural beauty.

In cooperation with the members of his psychoanalytic institute, but mainly with the help of his

pupil Michael Maccoby, he planned a new, sociopsychological field-research project in the Mexican state of Morelos. The project was to be financed with American research funds. As with his research project during the 'thirties on workers and employees in Mexico, the interaction of lifestyle and character structure was to be investigated by means of a questionnaire.

On the 11th of April, 1970, Fromm wrote to the Russian Philosopher Dobrenkov: "The interaction between socioeconomic factors and psychological and 'characterological factors' is studied in detail."

Above: Erich Fromm in Chiconuac among his Mexican students with whom he carried out the field research. Right, beside Fromm, Arturo Higareda and Alfonso Millán.

Talking to Jorge Velasco and Leonardo Santarelli; Alfonso Millán in the background.

Unlike the earlier study, these analyses—carried out with Michael Maccoby (left)—used psychoanalytic methods of interpretation, as well as the statistical technique of quantifying factor analysis.

"We were able to show how the character of the peasants of this village of 800 inhabitants is formed by class situation, and how, secondarily, their character influences their economic behavior."

This field research was conceived also as collaborative social research. It was not enough to recognize the dependence on economic and social structures of the various character orientations. These connections were to be talked over with the farmers in an effort to overcome the negative effects of their conditioning—such as alcoholism, and so to bring about a change in attitudes.

The research was finished only at the end of the 'sixties and published in 1970 by Erich Fromm and Michael Maccoby under the title *Social Character in a Mexican Village. A Sociopsychoanalytic Study*. The technique of participatory social research introduced at that time was later continued not only by Michael Maccoby in the U.S.A. and in Sweden, but also by the Mexican Seminario Sociopsicoanalítico under the directive of Salvador Millán and Sonia Gojman de Millán.

141

From 1953, Fromm was more in New York again. He rented a penthouse— 14b—at 180 Riverside Drive in New York City. He bought this apartment in 1962 and rented it out to his sister-in-law, Nita Hagan.

In the 'fifties and 'sixties Erich Fromm felt at home in Mexico, but he nevertheless considered himself American and remained a citizen of the United Sates until his death. Each year from 1953 he lived for several months outside Mexico, mostly in the U.S.A., then later increasingly in Europe.

After Henny's death he took up his teaching duties in 1953 again at the William Alanson White Institute and the New School for Social Research. New work opportunities with universities presented themselves: from 1956 he offered a regular series of lectures at the Kaufman Auditorium in New York, and the Young Men's and Young Women's Hebrew Association. From 1957 onwards he held seminars twice a year as Professor for Psychology in East Lansing at Michigan State University and, from 1962 onwards, he was adjunct professor at New York University.

Increasingly present in the United States again, in 1953 he rented a new flat in an attractive location overlooking the Hudson River at 180 Riverside Drive and gave up the apartment at 322 Central Park West, which he had rented after marrying Henny. The house they had built in Bennington was sold in 1955.

Spring and autumn usually found him in the U.S.A. for two or three months, partially in New York, sometimes on the lecture circuit. The more Fromm was known and the more he involved himself in American politics, the more he was in demand as a speaker. According to Fromm, in 1960 he received at least thirty invitations a month to lecture at American universities.

What made Fromm so attractive as a speaker? The issues he talked about were rather different. On the one hand he talked about the psychological issues that occupied him. At the beginning of the 'sixties, for example, he would speak about his research on narcissism and necrophilia (which was published eventually in 1964 as *The Heart of Man. Its Genius for Good and Evil*). On the other hand he stepped increasingly into the limelight as a political psychoanalyst and devoted his energies in favor of a communitarian, or rather humanistic socialism, developed so-called real utopias—models for reshaping the economy and society (as in *The Sane Society*, 1955) and persuaded the Socialist Party–Social Democratic Federation of the United States to adopt a new program.

In 1957, Fromm cofounded the most significant American peace movement SANE ("National Committee for a Sane Nuclear Policy"), fought passionately against the arms race and the nuclear armament and tried through his lectures to win over students and others to a policy of *détente* and disarmament.

Without Beatrice ("Trixi") Mayer, who was Fromm's secretary in Mexico, his international contacts and numerous publications would never have been possible. She not only typed the manuscripts for his books, but also his monthly correspondence of about 200 letters.

During his annual stays in the United States, Fromm undertook an extensive series of lectures.
In 1961 and 1962 alone he lectured at Allegheny, Amherst, Bennington, Brooklyn, Marin, Colorado, Haverford, Rutgers, San Francisco State, Wabash, at the Hebrew Union College, at the Merryl Palmer School, and the universities of Berkeley, Brandeis, Columbia, Harvard, New Hampshire, Roosevelt, Stanford, Massachusetts, Puerto Rico and Washington.

From the 9th to the 14th of July, 1962, Fromm and Homer A. Jack were invited by the president of the World Council of Peace, J. D. Bernal, to represent the anticommunist American peace movement, the National Committee for a Sane Nuclear Policy, at a peace congress in Moscow, to make a statement on disarmament. Fromm used his twenty-minute speech in the presence of Khrushchev to explain why disarmament proposals had failed. He spoke out for the recognition of China and the Oder-Neisse Line (the border between East Germany and Poland) and against nuclear armament of West Germany. Fromm also used this conference to arrange the release of his great-cousin Heinz Brandt, who had been kidnapped in 1961 in West Berlin, from imprisonment in the German Democratic Republic.

COUNCIL FOR CORRESPONDENCE

NEWSLETTER

in the tradition of

THE AMERICAN REVOLUTIONARY COMMITTEES OF CORRESPONDENCE

No. 23   February, 1963

THE GRAND DESIGN

Nations which unlike the United States have long military traditions and unchallenged ruling elites often excel in strategy but not in tactics. Freed from the need to explain and defend each strategic move to an independent Congress which pays the bills, those who govern can take

From 1960, together with David Riesman, Roger Hagen, and Michael Maccoby, Fromm published a collection of correspondence under the title *Council for Correspondence Newsletter*, which contained analysis of current political questions from a psychological perspective. They were addressed to congress-men, senators, and journalists. Fromm dealt mainly with the Soviet Union, China, and the question of the divided city of Berlin. But he also wrote on the Cuban crisis, the assassination of U.S. president Kennedy and developments in Israel. He found a receptive listener in Senator William Fulbright, Chairman of the powerful Foreign Relations Committee, with whom he maintained friendly contact until the late 'seventies.

Fromm at one of his numerous lectures in the U.S.A. In May 1966, over a period of three weeks in California, he reached an audience of 60,000. His fame in the U.S.A. during the 'sixties had its impact in Mexico, too. In October 1964, he lectured in Mexico City to an audience of over 3,000.

In 1961 Fromm published *May Man Prevail? An Inquiry into the Facts and Fictions of Foreign Policy*, in which he analyzed the Cold War noting that both countries use the same projections to experience the other as an enemy and arguing for an end to this dangerous confrontation—almost thirty years before it actually happened.

Fromm was in great demand because of his themes, his books, and his engagement with public policy. The charged political atmosphere of the 'sixties, especially the search for new perspectives by the younger generation, doubtless contributed to his popularity.

Fromm's special characteristic as a speaker was that he spoke "from the depth of his heart"—he wanted to communicate something and was interested in his listeners. As in personal conversations and during therapeutic sessions, he had the ability to connect directly with people.

The effect was overwhelming: On the 21st of November, 1960, Fromm wrote to Karl Polanyi, that he had spoken in favor of the Socialist Party at Yale University to 1200 students and at Chicago University to 2000 students. In November 1964 he told Clara Urquhart about a lecture journey with twenty-five stops and altogether more then 50,000 listeners. In some places thousands were unable to get in to hear him.

"Especially the young generation gave me the impression of freshness, openness, and hope, and of being really eager to hear somebody who had not too many illusions and yet faith."

Steven S. Schwarzschild, Professor of Philosophy and Judaic Studies at Washington University remembers: "When he came to Washington University in November 1967 for a week-long symposium, so many students flocked around him that loudspeakers had to be set up outside Graham Chapel for the overflow crowd to hear him."[65]

It was clear that Fromm had become the leading figure of a generation pushing for social change. Little wonder that the FBI had accumulated a file on him that ran to over 600 pages. [66]

The more famous Fromm became through his writing and public engagements, the more influence he had with other political lobbies: here a public appeal to politicians and statesmen, there a signature to a resolution. He joined many political movements and took part in various initiatives and interest groups. He frequently wrote letters to the newspapers.[67]

Concerns about world peace led him to contact other personalities of a humanistic persuasion, in order to plan events. As early as the late 'forties he had persuaded Albert Einstein, Martin Buber, and Leo Baeck to publish a declaration in the *New York Times* demanding respect for the rights of the Arabs as the state of Israel was founded.

At the beginning of the 'fifties he met several times with presidential candidate Adlai Stevenson. At the same time, he contacted Clarence Pickett, Stewart Meacham and other representatives of the American Friends' Service (the Quakers), who engaged

themselves in the peace movement. Fromm maintained a regular correspondence for years with Lewis Mumford, radical social critic and author of *The Myth of the Machine, Techniques and Human Development*. He also wrote to the Indian Prime Minister, Jawaharlal Nehru and met the British writer Aldous Huxley and the philosopher Betrand Russell.

During his occasional activities with the Socialist Party of the United States, Fromm cooperated with Norman Thomas and Karl Polanyi. He corresponded for many years with Raya Dunayevskaya, former secretary of Leon Trotski. Less intensive but equally warm was his exchange of letters with "Comrade" Angelica Balabanoff in Rome.

For some considerable time in the 'sixties, Fromm sought to organize a movement of humanist socialists, making contact with Ernst Bloch, Iring Fetscher, Lucien Goldman, Maximilien Rubel, Mathilde Niel, Tom Bottomore, Norman Birnbaum, Bertrand Russell, Léopold Senghor, Adam Schaff, Leszek Kolakowski, Milan Pruha, and Milan Machovec. He also made contacts with the philosophers of the "Praxis" Group in what was then Yugoslavia (Gajo Petrovic, Mihailo Markovic, Ljuba Stojic, Svetozar Stojanovic, Rudi Supek, and Predrag Vranicki). These manifold contacts are reflected in the anthology *Socialist Humanism*, an International Symposium, which Fromm published in 1965.

For Fromm, humanist socialism was the most important alternative to Western capitalism and to soviet-style communism. Fromm considered the latter even more inhumane then the Western economic system. On the 14th of April, 1960, he wrote to Karl Polanyi: "I am more strongly convinced than ever that the spiritual content in socialism, and especially in the ideas which Marx expressed in the Paris manuscripts are still as vital as they were a hundred years ago."

Fromm finally convinced Tom Bottomore, professor at the London School of Economics, to translate parts of Marx's early writings into English. He himself wrote an extensive introduction, and published Karl Marx's early writings under the title *Marx's Concept of Man* for the first time in the Anglo-Saxon world in 1961.

Erich Fromm talking to
Monsignor Leopold
Ungar in May 1967
during a Pacem in Terris
conference in Geneva.

Fromm was mainly attracted to Marx's "vision of socialism which expressed, in secular form, the idea of human self-realization, of total humanization, the idea of a human being whose goal is vital self-expression and not the acquisition and accumulation of dead, material things."[4]

To the Polish socialist Adam Schaff, Fromm wrote on the 8th of May, 1962: "I have been a socialist since my student days forty years ago, but have never been active politically until the last five years, when I have been very active in helping to form an American peace movement, on the left-wing of which I find myself."

Fromm sought comrades-in-arms for his humanistic alternative not only on the left. In the beginning of the 'sixties he also got in touch with engaged Catholics such as the Brazilian Archbishop Dom Helder Camara, the Trappist monk Thomas Merton, the professor of dogmatics, and Jesuit Karl Rahner and the Archbishop of Vienna, Cardinal König.

In 1963 he developed plans for a magazine to be called *Humanist Studies*, in which he wanted to bring humanists of different colors together but it never came to fruition. According to a letter of the18th of

September, 1963, the publishers were to be the Catholics Karl Rahner and Jean Daniélou and the Protestants Albert Schweitzer and Paul Tillich. Philosophy and science were to be represented by Bertrand Russell and Robert Oppenheimer, the Marxist side by Adam Schaff and Fromm. Buddhism was to be represented by Daisetz T. Suzuki and another Buddhist who was still to be named.

In 1966 Fromm tried (in vain), to persuade Pope Paul VI to call an international conference in which personalities from all over the world were to make suggestions as to how to enable humanity to survive. The Pope did not support this initiative, however, and it failed.

His last major political engagement was in 1968, when Fromm, as a sixty-eight-year-old, actively took part in the campaign of the Democratic Senator Eugene McCarthy for nomination as a presidential candidate. He traveled the length and breadth of the U.S.A. undertaking countless speeches and election events.

Once again he tried to use this opportunity to found a fundamental democratic movement, a *Revolution of*

Together with Norman Thomas, Erich Fromm received this peace prize in October 1963 in Chicago. It was awarded to the "psychoanalyst, sociologist, historian, and social commentator" (Fromm), "who has dispelled many of the dangerous myths of our age, given us rich insights into human conflict and conduct, and thereby illuminated pathways to world peace and understanding."

Hope, as he called his book which developed out of this election campaign. But with the failure of McCarthy to gain nomination, he gave up his attempt actively to influence American society and politics.

What motivated the social psychologist Fromm, educator of Mexican psychoanalysts and researcher into the social structure in a Mexican farmers village, to engage himself politically to such an extent in the United States?

For those who knew Fromm and experienced his alertness and emotional intensity both in conversation and in his political and social engagement, this is not a question: it was clear that Fromm had a kind of seismographic perception for all the contradictions, tensions and threats of humankind. Considering the vital role of the U.S.A. in international affairs, he sought to have some influence on political decision making in his adopted country.

Fromm was united with Albert Schweitzer in his struggle against the nuclear threat and in the concept of "respect for life," which has much in common with Fromm's concept of the "love of life" (biophilia) developed in the 'sixties.

Fromm maintained correspondence for many years with Clara Urquhart, the British writer. It was she who introduced him to Albert Schweitzer.

In a letter to Clara Urquhart, Fromm wrote on the 29th of September, 1962: "The other night I wrote a kind of appeal which is centered around the love of life. It was born out of a mood of despair which made me feel that there is hardly any chance that atomic war will be avoided, and sudden insight in which I felt that the reason why people are so passive toward the dangers of war lies in the fact that the majority just do not love life. I thought that to appeal to their love of life rather than to their love of peace or to their fear of war might have more impact."

The letter not only demonstrates Fromm's empathy for humanity. It marks the birth of an insight that he developed intensively over the following ten years, the significance and relevance of which has perhaps become clearer today.

Fromm observed that fewer and fewer people were attracted to life and liveliness, and more to the destructive and the dead, often seeking out destruction for its own sake.

The Arms Race and the worsening of the Cold War between the United States and the Soviet Union heightened the possibility of an atomic war at the beginning of the 'sixties–especially during the Cuban

Crisis of October 1962. This threatening international situation troubled Fromm greatly. His domestic bliss was also under threat at this time: his wife was diagnosed as suffering from breast cancer (which was fortunately overcome by an operation and a drastic diet). These concerns, combined with his experiences as a therapist, prompted Fromm to pursue research into the psychological roots of destructiveness.

Back in 1920, Freud hypothesized in his drive theory that the urge to destroy is caused by a death drive, which springs from the same source as the survival instinct.

Differing from Freud, Fromm held on to the idea, based on biological considerations, that: "the preservation of life is the supreme biological law"[4] and so all life has the primary tendency to grow and develop and that the destructive in humans has its roots in the hindrance and the obstruction of this inherent law.

"We can demonstrate that destructive tendencies–tendencies growing out of the death instinct–result from failures in the art of living. They are the consequences of not living correctly."[4]
The hypothesis that destructive behavior is not

We can show that people who have no chance to be free and to develop their own powers, people who are hemmed in, who live in a class or society in which everything functions in a mechanical, lifeless way—these people lose their capacity to "sparkle."[4]

determined by a natural law, but comes from living inappropriately is valid with one important caveat: Fromm also accepted, of course, that human beings naturally display that type of aggression that is necessary for survival: the reaction to threat and fear.

Within this "reactive" aggression, which humans share with animals, certain forms of aggression have to be distinguished, namely, those that have developed historically. Such human aggression has its roots within the character of those who constantly need to act out their hostility toward others and actively seek out their victims.

The necrophilic character can manifest itself directly in fascination with that which is dead, deathly, destructive, bad-smelling, dirty, or rotten. Such a character may manifest itself indirectly, however, by being attracted to all that is deeply clean, or has a shining, lifeless surface, is purely cerebral or possesses a soulless regularity. This latter manifestation of necrophilia seeks ideal forms, freed from the vicissitudes of life, the ambivalence of feelings, the becoming and the dying.

Sadists, who enjoy dominating, torturing and humiliating others, are known everywhere. This form of destructivity seems to be inherent in such individuals' characters. Previously, in the 'thirties, Fromm had dealt with the authoritarian character and he returned to this theme in 1973 with *The Anatomy of Human Destructiveness*, in which he developed his argument using Heinrich Himmler as an example.

At the beginning of the 'sixties Fromm discovered a second character-oriented destructivity, which he called "necrophilia" (from the Greek *nekros* = dead, corpse). Similarly to sadism, necrophilia has many aspects. One common factor is that necrophilic persons are more attracted to the dead than to the living. They continually try to kill things, to turn the organic into inorganic, split up the whole into parts, use up consumables, turn living things into objects.

The discovery that people were becoming attracted

more to death than to life in increasing numbers seemed at first peculiar to Fromm. So he sent the relevant chapter of his book to several scientists for evaluation before he published his findings in *The Heart of Man*, 1964.

The question of destructiveness and specifically of necrophilia continued to fascinate him. For five years, between 1968 and 1973 he again concentrated entirely on the question of aggression, work that bore fruit in *The Anatomy of Human Destructiveness*.

In 1965, Fromm was granted emeritus status at the University of Mexico, but he made no plans to reduce his scientific work load, nor to retire from his international engagements. Freed from educational duties in Mexico, he intended to write a four volume work on his understanding of psychoanalysis in theory and practice. But it was not to be. At the beginning of December 1966 the peace organization, SANE unexpectedly invited him to give a speech at a big rally in Madison Square Gardens, New York, in favor of peace in Vietnam. Breaking with his habit of traveling to New York in the Pullman compartment of a train, he flew there and filled the rest of his week in New York with appointments. Fromm—aged sixty-six—suffered his first heart attack, which confined him to bed for ten weeks. He had to abandon work for many months.

In this situation he traveled with Annis by sea to Europe. They went to Baden Baden, and for further treatment to Freiburg-Breisgau. Later, they visited his cousin, Gertrud Hunziker-Fromm in Zürich and spent some weeks at the Hotel Muralto in Locarno. It was nine months before they returned to Mexico in the autumn of 1967. From then on, they spent only the winter months in Cuernavaca, living in Europe during the summer. From the 1st of July, 1969, they rented an apartment at 4 Via Franscini in Locarno-Muralto and, in mid-1974, they decided never to return to Mexico.

The Mexican caricaturist, Oswaldo, summarized the various aspects of Fromm's personality rather well: a big head with huge therapist's ears and bright eyes on a small, rather weak body; in his left hand, the flowers of the lover, in the right a few books; always under way and leaving traces of love to life.

7
Life out of Being:
The Wisdom of Old Age

"There is a Hasidic story which occurs to me. The pupil
sees the rabbi in a sad mood and asks him: 'Master why
are you sad? Are you sad that have you not reached
the highest knowledge, that you have not the greatest
virtues?' The master said: 'No, I am not sad about that.
I am sad not to have become myself totally.'

That is to say, in every human being there is an opti-
mum of what he could become, there are things that he
could never become. So many people waste their lives
by trying to become what they could not be and by
neglecting to be what they could become. So a person
in the first place should have a certain image of what
he could and what he could not become, what are the
limitations and what are the possibilities."[1]

Joan Hughes, Fromm's secretary during his time in Locarno, took everything with dry English humor and tirelessly typed everything that Fromm wrote by hand, or dictated for correspondence.

The special climate of Ticino was not the only factor that persuaded Annis and Erich Fromm not to return to Mexico after 1973. The following summer, when Fromm made a definite decision for Locarno this was also a letting go of the responsibility for his now "grown-up" students in Mexico and a return to his European homeland.

He had most of his library, his correspondence, and his manuscripts sent to Locarno. The house in Cuernavaca was sold in 1976 without his ever returning to Mexico.

Fromm wanted to be free for a new project, which had already taken shape in his mind shortly after he had finished his book on human destructiveness. On the 8th of April, 1974, he wrote to Lewis Mumford, with whom he had been in contact since the mid-'fifties:

"I am happy to go on with my writing on the topic 'To Have Or to Be?' which is an analysis of two modes of existence, the one in which the world is perceived in terms of an object of having and the other in which what matters is the act of living itself, of productive work, of the unfolding of human capacities and in which the sense of identity is not based on the formula 'I am what I have' but 'I am what I do,' 'doing' here not in the sense of superficial activity but of authentic, productive activity."

Offering his readers the choice "To Have Or to Be", Fromm took up again the central theme of his psychoanalytic theory that he had sought to explain in

"This place, Locarno, has a certain unreality [concerning] the world; it produces a feeling of peace and beauty which is extraordinary."[68]

From 1969 on, Annis and Erich Fromm spent the summer in "Casa La Monda," the apartment building at 4 Via Franscini in Locarno, Muralto, Switzerland, and from 1974 they stayed there all year round. Rainer Funk (here with Fromm on a walk in March, 1979) became Fromm's assistant in 1974 and later his literary executor.

Man for Himself (1947), by differentiating between productive and non productive character orientation.

Throughout life, the processes of thinking, feeling, and acting confirm and reinforce the tendencies of psychological systems to develop or atrophy. The primary tendency of that psychological system that seeks to develop can be crippled and obstructed if the human being relies not on his own mental, psychic, and physical strength, but on forces and values, things, people, and qualities that he acquires from outside himself.

Those psychological drives and orientations that result from the forces within a human being Fromm calls "being oriented" or "productive," since they are produced from within one's inner forces. The others he calls non productive, or oriented toward "having," because they are from outside and only appear to be our own.

Those things which someone oriented toward "having" possesses are not really his, but rather a compensation for a lack of "being." This becomes clear as soon as these possessions are taken from him. The loss of the possessions is experienced as a loss of self. Not only may such a person lose his property, his life partner, his honor, or his good conscience, he also may lose the ground beneath his feet, that on which he based his "being."

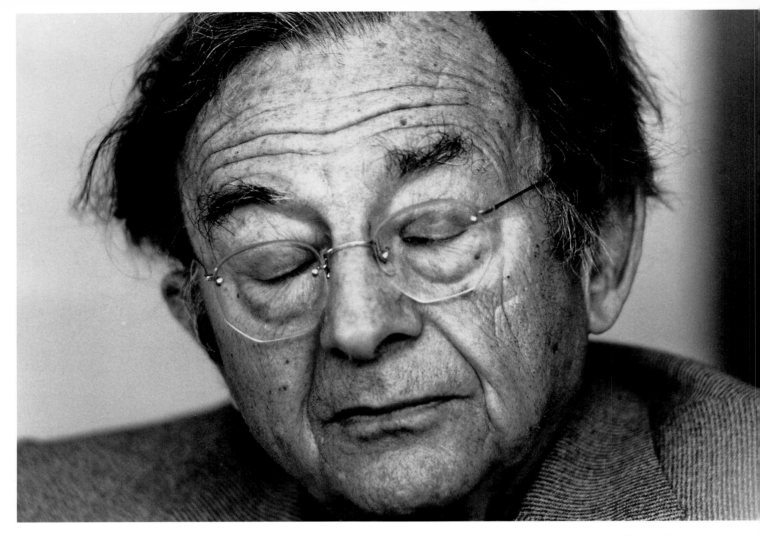

Naturally, the "being-oriented" person also experiences the loss of someone close, the loss of a job or of his reputation as painful. He does not, however, experience it as annihilation. He is more than what he posesses because his being is based on his own inner strength.

Inner strength–being able to love, to concentrate, to be tender, joyful, and sad, to be sympathetic and to know how to demarcate oneself–all these abilities develop through practice and become stronger if they are shared. They are psychological growth factors and follow a totally different pattern from the "having" orientation. The latter are acquired from outside and are consumed and lost when they are used and shared–they are thus non productive.

The choice "To Have Or to Be?" refers to modes of existence and characterizes their productive or non-productive impact on the human system–a system designed primarily for growth. Psychologically speaking, it is about the strengthening or hindrance of this inherent urge to grow. This should be borne in mind so as to avoid misunderstanding what this choice involves.

The question of what a human being possesses or does not possess is not the most important consideration, but whether a person bases his being on possessions. So trying to overcome the "having orientation" does not necessarily involve asceticism, the renunciation of life, or reorientation toward abstention from possessions, rather the summoning and practicing of inner strength.

Being with the other...

Although *To Have Or to Be?* was published as long ago as 1976, only now are its penetrating ideas beginning to have their impact. That system of production we call the market economy has now become almost exclusively determined by the "philosophy of marketing." What counts is not the utility value of a product or of a service, but its marketability and its marketing—a successful sales strategy.

Supply and demand no longer regulate the market as they once did; demand is created and artificially manipulated through "lifestyle marketing" which attaches to brands and suggests to the consumer that, by being associated with a particular brand, he will become truly alive, feel at home, experience satisfaction or happiness, and become attractive, interesting, loving, and self-aware.

The particular characteristics of an individual, which are naturally brought into being through inherent human forces, are reassigned to products, or to the stage-managed life experience of the Coca-Cola, MacDonalds, or Nike worlds. To orient oneself toward "having" inevitably means defining oneself through what cannot be realized from within. This mind-set has in the meantime come to characterize the entire economy and all realms of life.

A person's own Ego has become a product to be had; one receives training in how to to sell oneself. Being an integrated and authentic person is no longer the goal: possessing the right personality profile is what counts. It is of vital importance to make oneself attractive, sell oneself successfully, portray oneself in the right light, to present oneself with focused self-confidence. It is of no longer of interest what feelings one has and who one really is.

"The aim of modern society is not the realization of the human being, but profit; not profit in the sense of greed, but in the sense of maximum efficiency of the economic system. Most importantly, profit is a signal of the most rational and correct management. The manager who makes a profit shows that he has managed the business rationally and the higher the profit, the better, the more right, the more rational."[2]

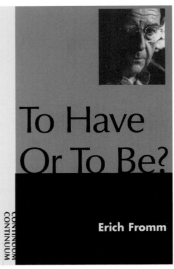

To Have Or to Be? was published in 1976. In Germany, Italy, and elsewhere, it achieved the status of a cult book for a generation that was still searching for alternatives.

To Have Or To Be?

CONTINUUM
CONTINUUM

Erich Fromm

"I believe, indeed, that our society offers the picture of a low grade chronic schizophrenia. The fact is that most people today are employees high or low [who] do what they are told or what the rules tell them and feel as little as possible because feelings disturb the smooth functioning of the machine. People must train themselves to have as [few] emotions as possible because an emotion costs money."[1]

Not only is the outer reality stage-managed, one's own identity experience also becomes manipulated reality. Such a reality—oriented toward "having"—becomes a more and more attractive alternative to recognizing and shaping reality by "being".

New in Fromm's choice of "To Have Or to Be?" is not the choice itself, but its application to a marketing oriented society. He discovered the choice had already been formulated by the medieval mystic, Meister Eckhart, and by Karl Marx.

Fromm wrote chapter after chapter of his new book with great enthusiasm, handing it to his secretary, Joan Hughes, to be typed, and then read to his wife Annis, his assistant, Rainer Funk, and his cousin Gertrud Hunziker-Fromm in Zurich. Their opinions often led him to rewrite whole paragraphs, develop new ideas or redesign the concept of the book. Sometimes, by the time he received their feedback, he had already rewritten a chapter, feeling that what he had written did not really express what he felt.[69]

The longer Fromm lived in Ticino, the more his work became known there. As early as 1969 and 1970, Oskar Schatz from Austrian radio invited Fromm to give the "Salzburg talks on humanism." Hans Jürgen Schultz, who covered news of resorts for South German radio in Stuttgart, "discovered" Fromm in 1970 and arranged for him to give a series of radio lectures, and Hans Lechleitner from German television and Heiner

Gautschy of Swiss-German television introduced Fromm to a wide audience and so contributed to Fromm's book *To Have Or to Be?* achieving cult status, selling many millions of copies.

Fromm was not that interested in public relations, however. He preferred to exchange ideas with friends and guests who came for visits to Locarno and to whom he was always a generous host. Among these were Katya Delakova and her husband Moshe Budmor; his great-cousin Heinz Brandt, whose release from a concentration camp Fromm managed to obtain in 1940 and later, between 1961 and 1964 from imprisonment in East Germany. Albert Speer, chief architect of the Third Reich, came to visit several times to talk about Hitler. Professional colleagues were regular visitors: Michael Maccoby, Marianne Horney Eckardt, David Schecter, Jorge Silva, and other former psychoanalytic students from the U.S.A. and Mexico. The social reformer Danilo Dolci came from Sicily, Ivan Illich from Mexico, and Ernst Simon, his lifelong friend from Israel and member of the "Praxis" group of philosophers from the former Yugoslavia.

During his annual visits to Locarno, Nyanaponika Mahathera trained Fromm in Buddhist concentration and meditation exercises which the psychoanalyst undertook daily between eleven o'clock and noon.

Boris Luban-Plozza from Ascona, who worked with the Balint movement to improve understanding between physicians and their patients, often came to seek Fromm's advice. In 1975, with Rainer Funk, he arranged a major symposium to mark Fromm's seventy-fifth birthday in the Muralto congress hall.

Max Kreutzberger, previously director of the New York Leo Baeck Institute, also retired to Locarno and was a regular visitor. Through Kreutzberger, Fromm came to know Nyanaponika Mahathera, the Buddhist teacher from Sri Lanka.

After the publication of *To Have Or to Be?* Fromm became almost as well known in Europe as he had been during the 'sixties in America. He gave interviews for British, Dutch, and Italian television and to journalists from all over Europe and even during his holidays at the Waldhaus Hotel in Vulpera (Engadin, Switzerland), at the Hotel Bellevue in Baden Baden or at the Adler-Post Hotel in Hinterzarten in the Black Forest.

In 1975, Fromm attended a conference on Albert Schweitzer in Paris. Disturbed by the political persecution of the Yugoslav "Praxis" philosophers, Fromm contacted Ernst and Karola Bloch, Heinrich Böll, and the Yugoslav ambassadors in Washington and many other countries, hoping to persuade Josip Tito to back down. For Senator Fulbright, he wrote an expert opinion on the policy of *détente*. When he was invited by the attorney Klaus Croissant to appear as a witness for the defense in the German Bader-Meinhoff terrorist trial in 1976, however, Fromm rejected the idea.

Fromm believed that the exiled Russian novelist Aleksandr Solzhenitsyn was promoting the Cold War so he attempted to gather support for a declaration denouncing his position. He contacted Tristram Coffin,

publisher of the *Washington Spectator*, Noam Chomsky, William Fulbright, David Riesman, Lewis Mumford, and Michael Maccoby. He failed to gather the necessary support but the attempt demonstrates how much he was again engaging himself politically.

This greater engagement had an influence on his health. In mid-1975, he suffered severe pain in his gallbladder and was hospitalized, first in Locarno, then in Zurich. In 1975, he had gallstones removed at a New York hospital where he stayed for ten weeks. On the 7th of November, 1975, he wrote to Lewis Mumford:

"The illness was an interesting and fruitful experience. I had little pain and the occasion to meditate and analyze myself practically the whole day."

Bernard Landis, a New York psychoanalyst, came to Locarno in the summer of 1974 with psychology students from New York for a two-week seminar with Fromm. Out of the transcript of this seminar grew *The Art of Listening* which was published posthumously.

Katya Delakova instructed Fromm in Tai Chi and similar exercises. The dancer and choreographer, born in Vienna, had worked with Moshe Feldenkrais and specialized in such Eastern exercise systems. She visited Fromm regularly with her husband, Moshe Budmor.

Fromm's cousin, Gertrud Hunziker-Fromm, the psychoanalyst from Zurich, and her husband, the painter Max Hunziker, maintained warm relations.

Above: In June 1976 Wolfgang Zander from Munich came with a group of German psychoanalysts for a therapeutic seminar with Fromm on the Monte Verità, Ascona.

Above: The communities of Locarno and Muralto honored Fromm in February 1980 with a celebration in the Locarno *Kursaal*, in which Ivan Illich gave the encomium. Fromm had meanwhile been awarded the Dortmund Nelly Sachs Prize and was made an honorary citizen of Muralto. Perhaps for once, Ivan Illich is telling a Hasidic joke.

In the late summer of 1977, Fromm suffered a second heart attack that forced him to abandon all his plans for the rest of the year. Just as he had recovered, in spring 1978, he suffered a third heart attack—this time a severe one. He had a pacemaker implanted in Zurich. Now he could read only with difficulty and his short-term memory suffered for several months. At the end of 1979, however, his health improved. In February 1980, he celebrated his eightieth birthday early in the Kursaal of Locarno and was also able to give a few interviews.

Five days before his actual birthday, in the morning of the 18th of March, he suffered another heart attack: this time it was fatal. Ivan Illich organized a small ceremony in the crematorium at Bellinzona. Fromm had not wanted a grave. His ashes were to be scattered over the waters of Lago Maggiore.

At the end of 1982 Annis Fromm left Switzerland and returned to Montgomery, Alabama. There she died in September 1985.

Shortly before his death Fromm said in an interview:

"It is a strange thing, most people believe that in order to live a good life, one has not to practice."[1]

For Fromm, life was not to be taken for granted but also a task assigned. For him, it was not always an easy task.

The art of living demands daily practice, using one's inner life force. This art is to be discovered both within oneself and in interaction with reality—often resisted by the "pathology of normalcy," disguised as "common sense."

The aim of the art of living is to be connected with the outer and inner realities and with one's own mental, psychic, and physical powers in such a way that the love of life may grow.

Notes

All of the quotations from the correspondence of Erich Fromm are taken from the Erich Fromm Archive in Tübingen, administered by Dr. Rainer Funk.

Citations from the work of Erich Fromm are taken from *Erich Fromm Gesamtausgabe in zwölf Bänden*, edited by Rainer Funk, Stuttgart (Deutsche Verlags-Anstalt) and Munich (Deutscher Taschenbuch Verlag) 1999. Volumes I to X correspond to *Erich Fromm Gesamtausgabe in zehn Bänden*, edited by Rainer Funk, Stuttgart (Deutsche Verlags-Anstalt) 1980-81 and Munich (Deutscher Taschenbuch Verlag) 1989.

1 Interview with Gérard Khoury from Aix en Provence, 1978 and 1979, recorded in Locarno. Here quoted from the transcript. A part of the interview was published under the title "Erich Fromm: du Talmud à Freud"(1979d), in *Le Monde Dimanche*, Paris (21.10.1979), p. xv.

2 Interview with Guido Ferrari of Swiss television in Ticino, recorded shortly before Fromm's death in March 1980 in Locarno; here quoted from the transcript of the interview conducted in German.

3 From a TV interview with Jürgen Lodemann and Micaela Lämmle from Südwestrundfunk in Baden Baden 1977, conducted in Locarno.

4 From an interview with Hans Jürgen Schultz, conducted in 1973 and published in *For the Love of Life* (1983a, New York: The Free Press, 1986).

5 E. Fromm, *Beyond the Chains of Illusion. My Encounter with Marx and Freud*, New York: Simon and Schuster, 1962, p. 3.

6 Hans Hayn in an interview, first published partially in 1990 in a television film directed by Rainer Otte und Stefan Fricke about Fromm's biography *Leben durch Geschichte*.

7 E. Fromm, *Beyond the Chains of Illusion*, pp. 3-4.

8 E. Fromm, *Beyond the Chains of Illusion*, p. 4.

9 E. Fromm, *Beyond the Chains of Illusion*, p. 6.

10 "Prophets and Priests" in: *Bertrand Russell. Philosopher of the Century: Essays in His Honor*, R. Schoenman (Ed.): London: George Allen and Unwin, 1967, pp. 67-79, (here pp. 67-68.).

11 Obituary for Rabbi Nobel in the *Jüdische Rundschau* from the 31st of January, 1922.

12 You Shall Be as Gods. A Radical Interpretation of the Old Testament and Its Tradition (1966a), New York: Holt, Rinehart and Winston, 1966, p. 13.

13 L. Löwenthal, *Mitmachen wollte ich nie. Ein autobiographisches Gespräch mit Helmut Dubiel*, Frankfurt: Suhrkamp, 1980, p. 20.

14 F. Rosenzweig, letter from the 14th of April, 1919 to his mother in: *Briefe und Tagebücher*, Vol. 2: 1918-29, Haag: Martinus Nijhoff, 1979, p. 627.

15 Vgl. B. Ostrovsky, in: *Jüdisches Leben in Deutschland*, Vol. 3: *Selbstzeugnisse zur Sozialgeschichte 1918-45*, Stuttgart: Deutsche Verlags-Anstalt, 1982.

16 Letter of Ernst Simon to Martin Buber dated the11th of December, 1922, printed in: *Sechzig Jahre gegen den Strom. Ernst A. Simon. Briefe von 1917-84*, Ed. Leo Baeck Institute, Jerusalem, Tübingen: Mohr Siebeck, 1998, p. 22.

17 G. Scholem, *Walter Benjamin-die Geschichte einer Freundschaft*, Frankfurt: Suhrkamp, 1975, S. 149.

18 Letter to Lewis Mumford from the 29th of April, 1975.

19 *Erinnerungen von Rabbiner Dr. Georg Salzberger über das "Freie Jüdische Lehrhaus,"* Program from Radio Free Berlin on the 4th of August,1974. Cf. also "Die Gesellschaft für jüdische Volksbildung in Frankfurt am Main," in: *Bulletin of the Leo Baeck Institute*, New York Vol. 10 (1967, No. 37-40), pp. 80-88.

20 W. Schivelbusch, *Intellektuellen-dämmerung. Zur Frage der Frankfurter Intelligenz in den zwanziger Jahren*, Frankfurt: Insel Verlag, 1982, p. 30.

21 Quoted from a circular letter to "die verehrlichen Platzinhaber der Synagoge Unterlindau" (honored seat holders in the Unterlindau Synagogue) on the first anniversary of the death of Naphtali Fromm, in which contributions were sought for the foundation of an "eternal light in honor of the deceased" (Erich Fromm Archive, Tübingen).

22 From a letter to Lewis Mumford from the 29th of April, 1975.

23 Erich Fromm in his "Reminiscences of Shlomo Barukh Rabinkow" Ed. Jacob J. Schacter, in: *Sages and Saints*, Ed. Jung, L., (The Jewish Library: Vol. 10), Hoboken: Ktav Publishing House, Inc., 1987, pp. 99-105.

24 It was not until 1989 that Erich Fromm's dissertation was published, in volume 2 of his hitherto unpublished works: *Das jüdische Gesetz. Zur Soziologie des Diaspora-Judentums. Dissertation von 1922*, Ed. Rainer Funk and Bernd Sahler, Weinheim and Basel (Beltz Verlag) 1989; republished in Vol. 11 (additional volume) of the *Erich Fromm-Gesamtausgabe in zwölf Bänden*, Stuttgart: Deutsche Verlags-Anstalt, 1999 and München: Deutscher Taschenbuch Verlag, 1999. The quotation is taken from the 1989 edition, page 15. To date, the dissertation has been translated only into Italian.

25 Transcript of an autobiographical interview, conducted in 1954 in the U.S.A. Parts of it were published: "Frieda Fromm-Reichmann-Reminiscences of Europe," in: *Psychoanalysis and Psychosis*, Ed. A. L. Silver, Madison: International Universities Press, 1989, pp. 469-481.

26 From one typeset page of "Erinnerungen an Erich Fromm" by Ernst Simon, which is in the Institut für Stadtgeschichte, Frankfurt.

27 Frieda Fromm-Reichmann, "Das jüdische Speiseritual," in: *Imago*, Vol. 13 (1927), pp. 235-46; Erich Fromm, "Der Sabbath" (1927a), ibid., pp. 223-234.

28 E. Fromm, "Der Sabbath," 1927a, in: Imago, Vol. 13 (1927), p. 234.

29 Erich Fromm in a letter to Sylvia

Grossman from the12th of November 1957.

30 Quoted after Herbert Will, *Die Geburt der Psychosomatik. Georg Groddeck, der Mensch und Wissenchaftler*, München: Urban & Schwarzenberg, 1984, p. 22. .

31 Ingeborg Bachmann, "Entwurf zu Georg Groddeck," in *Werke*, published by Christine Koschel, Inge von Weidenbaum and Clemens Müller, Vol. 4, München: R. Piper, 1978, p. 351.

32 Erich Fromm's article was first published in *Zeitschrift für Psychoanalytische Pädagogik* (Vol. 3, 1929, pp. 268-70). An English translation was published under the title "Psychoanalysis and Sociology" in *Critical Theory and Society. A Reader*, Ed. S. E. Bronner and D. M. Kellner, New York and London: Routledge, 1989, pp. 37-39.

33 "Psychoanalysis and Sociology," 1929a, p. 39.

34 *The Dogma of Christ* (1930a), in: E. Fromm, *The Dogma of Christ and Other Essays on Religion, Psychology and Culture*, New York: Holt, Rinehartd and Winston, 1963a, p. 9.

35 Letter by Karl Landauer to Max Horkheimer from the 28th of January, 1941, printed in: Max Horkheimer, *Gesammelte Schriften*, Ed. Gunzelin Schmid Noerr, Vol. 16, p. 698.

36 Max Horkheimer in a letter to Sigmund Freud from the 18th of March, 1932, formerly thought missing but which I discovered among Fromm's papers at the New York Public Library .

37 From a lecture entitled "The Crisis of the Patriarchal Order," in: *For the Love of Live*, New York (The Free Press) 1986, pp. 21-22.

38 Most of the correspondence between Erich Fromm and Max Horkheimer has been published in: Max Horkheimer, *Gesammelte Schriften*, Ed. Alfred Schmidt and Gunzelin Schmid Noerr, in vols. 15-18, *Briefwechsel*, Ed. Gunzelin Schmid Noerr, Frankfurt am Main: S. Fischer Verlag, 1995 bis 1996. Quotations from the letters by Horkheimer and Karl Landauer have been taken out of these volumes.

39 Personal note.

40 Letter by Fromm from the 22nd of June, 1938, to Charles A. Pearce from Verlag Harcourt, Brace and Co. in New York.

41 In the context of the termination of Fromm's contract with the institute Fromm turned to the former Prussian minister of justice, Kurt Rosenfeld, who had emigrated as a lawyer in 1934 to New York, and asked him to mediate. On the 16th of November, 1939 Fromm handed a "memorandum" to him, in which Fromm described his cooperation with the institute and the circumstances of the termination of his contract. The quotations are taken from this memorandum.

42 Fromm's letter to Robert Lynd from the 1st of March, 1939.

43 All of the quotations are taken from the article in 1937 that had been missing and that I discovered only in 1991 in the New York Public Library. I published the article in 1992 under the title *Die Determiniertheit der psychischen Struktur durch die Gesellschaft. Zur Methode und Aufgabe einer Analytischen Sozialpsychologie* (1992e [1937]) in the publication *Gesellschaft und Seele* (Weinheim, Beltz Verlag 1992). In *Erich Fromm-Gesamtausgabe in zwölf Bänden* (Stuttgart: Deutsche Verlags-Anstalt, and München: Deutscher Taschenbuch Verlag, 1999) it appears in volume 11. The English text is currently available only on the home page of the International Erich Fromm Society at: www.erich-fromm.de.

44 Fromm in a letter to Martin Jay from the 14th of May, 1971. With this letter Fromm answered many questions that Martin Jay asked in his groundbreaking history of the Frankfurter Schule (*The Dialectical Imagination. A History of the Frankfurt School and the Institute of Social Research 1923-1950, London 1973*). The letter has meanwhile been published under the title "Ein Memorandum in eigener Sache" in *Erich Fromm und die Frankfurter Schule*, M. Kessler and R. Funk (Eds.): papers of the Stuttgart-Hohenheim international, inter-disciplinary symposia, 31st May-2nd June, 1991, Tübingen: Francke Verlag, 1992, pp. 249-256.

45 Letter to Leo Löwenthal on the 31st of October, 1942.

46 Th. W. Adorno, "Die revidierte Psychoanalyse," in: Sociologica II, Frankfurt: Suhrkamp, 1962, pp. 94-112, here p. 96.

47 Qutoted after J. L. Rubins, *Karen Horney. Sanfte Rebellin der Psycho-analyse. Eine Biographie*, München: Kindler, 1980, p. 216; 256; 255.

48 *Escape from Freedom*, New York: Farrar and Rinehart, 1941, p. 290.

49 G. Reichmann, quoted after the dissertation, that Angelika Schönhagen wrote under the title *Frieda Fromm-Reichmann. Leben und Werk* 1980 in Mainz, p. 27.

50 F. Fromm-Reichmann, *Principles of Intensive Psychotherapy*, Chicago: The University of Chicago Press, 1950.

51 J. Rattner, *Psychologie der zwischenmenschlichen Beziehungen*, Olten: Walter-Verlag, 1969, p. 19.

52 E. Fromm, *Die gesellschaftliche Bedingtheit der psychoanalytischen Therapie* (1935a), in: *Erich Fromm-Gesamtausgabe in zwölf Bänden* (Stuttgart: Deutsche Verlags-Anstalt, and München: Deutscher Taschenbuch Verlag, 1999), Vol. 1, p. 119, 131, 133-35.

53 E. Fromm, *Psychoanalysis and Zen Buddhism* (1960a), p. 112.

54 Fromm's most important publications on technical therapeutic questions are: *Psychoanalysis and Zen Buddhism* (1960a) in *Zen Buddhism and Psychoanalysis*, 1960, a short article *The Oedipus Complex: Comments on the "Case of Little Hans"* (1966k, in: E. Fromm, *The Crisis of Psychoanalysis*, 1970a), a lecture from 1954 under the title *Remarks on the Problem of Free Association* (1955d, in: Psychiatric Research Report, Washington, Vol. 2 (1955), pp. 1-6), three lectures in 1959, which were published only posthum under the title *Das Unbewußte und die psycho-analytische Praxis* (1992g [1959]) and have not been published in the English original so far; a lecture with the title *Factors Leading to Patient's Change in Analytic Treatment* (1991c [1964]), in: E. Fromm, *The Art of Listening*, New York: Continuum, 1992, pp. 15-41; the discourse *The Dialectic Revision of Psychoanalysis* (1990f [1969], in: E. Fromm, *The*

Revision of Psychoanalysis (Boulder: Westview Press 1992, pp. 19-80), which deal with the questions of therapeutic techniques in the last paragraphs, the recording of a psychoanalytical seminar with case examples from the year 1974 with the title *The Art of Listening* (1991d [1974]), New York: Continuum, 1992, pp. 45-193. To be mentioned is Fromm's German lecture "Die Bedeutung der Psychoanalyse für die Zukunft," (1992h [1975]), which he held on the symposium in Locarno on the occasion of his 75th birthday , as well as his book *The Forgotten Language* (1951a), which dealt with the symbolic language of the unconscious.

55 The English text of the "grundsätzlichen Aufsatz" from 1937, entitled *A Contribution to the Method and Purpose of an Analytical Social Psychology* is available on the website www.erich-fromm.de under the "Articles by Fromm" section. Cf. also note 43.

56 I explained and documented the history of Fromm's loss of his membership in the Deutschen Psychoanalytischen Gesellschaft (D.P.G.) (German Psychoanalytical Society) and the foundation of his own, nonorthodox umbrella organization, the International Federation of Psychoanalytic Societies (IFPS) in 1961, in the article "Erich Fromm's Role in the Foundation of the IFPS. Evidence from the Erich Fromm Archives in Tuebingen," in *Fromm Forum*, Ed. International Erich Fromm Society, (ISSN: 1437-1189), Tuebingen, Vol. 3 (1999), S. 17-27.

57 Bernard J. Paris, *Karen Horney. A Psychoanalyst's Search for Self-Understanding*, New Haven and London: Yale University Press, 1994, p. 155; 149; 147.

58 Quoted after WAWI (William Alanson White Institute) *Newsletter*, New York, Vol. 8 (No. 1, Autumn 1973), p. 2.

59 E. Fromm, *Sozialpsychologischer Teil* (1936a), *Erich Fromm-Gesamtausgabe in zwölf Bänden* (Stuttgart: Deutsche Verlags-Anstalt, and Munich: Deutscher Taschenbuch Verlag, 1999) Vol. 1, p. 172.

60 These were: Aniceto Aramoni, Giullermo Dávila, Jorge Derbez, José F. Díaz, Ramón de la Fuente, Abraham Fortes, Francisco Garcia, Raúl González, José Gutiérrez, Armando Hinojosa, Alfonso Millán, Jorge Silva und Jorge Velasco.

61 J. Silva, *Fromm in Mexico*: 1950-1973, in: *Contemporary Psychoanalysis*, New York Vol. 25 (1989), pp. 244-57, 248.

62 Erich Fromm in a letter to Suzuki from the 18th of October, 1956.

63 E. Fromm, *Humanism and Psychoanalysis* (1963f), in: *Contemporary Psychoanalysis*, New York Vol. 1 (1964), pp. 69-79, here p. 72; 77.

64 E. Fromm, *The Art of Loving. An Inquiry into the Nature of Love* (1956a), New York: Harper and Row, 1956, p. 103.

65 S. S. Schwarzschild, "Remembering Erich Fromm," in: *The Jewish Spectator*, Fall 1980, pp. 29-33, here p. 29.

66 Paul Roazen in a letter to the editor on the13th of September, 1992 of the Sunday editon of the *New York Times*.

67 Some of these activities have meanwhile been published in Vol. 11 of *Erich Fromm-Gesamtausgabe in zwölf Bänden* (Stuttgart: Deutsche Verlags-Anstalt, and München: Deutscher Taschenbuch Verlag, 1999).

68 Letter to Aniceto Aramoni from the 6th of June, 1977.

69 Most of the parts that had not been published by Fromm himself were posthumously published by Rainer Funk and are available in vols. 11 and 12 of *Erich Fromm-Gesamtausgabe in zwölf Bänden* (Stuttgart: Deutsche Verlags-Anstalt, and Munich: Deutscher Taschenbuch Verlag, 1999) Cf. also the titles *The Art of Being* (1989a) and *On Being Human*, (1992b). In the latter those chapters are also printed which deal in greater depth with the choice of "To Have Or to Be?" in Meister Eckhart and Karl Marx.

70 Fromm's articles were published in 1983 by Hans Jürgen Schultz in *For the Love of Life*.

Organizations Devoted to Erich Fromm

International Erich Fromm Society
The Erich Fromm Society was founded in 1985 and now has around 500 members worldwide. The society promotes the thought and works of Erich Fromm, organizes national and international seminars and conferences and publishes the annual *Fromm Forum* (German edition: ISSN 1437-0956; English edition: ISSN 1437-1189–available from the office of the Erich Fromm Association in Tübingen). Further information about membership is available on the website of the association at www.erich-fromm.de, and at the office:

Internationale Erich-Fromm-Gesellschaft e. V.
Ursrainer Ring 24
D – 72076 Tübingen
Telephone: +49(0)7071 - 600004;
Fax: +49(0)7071 - 600049;
Email: fromm@germanymail.com;
Website: www.erich-fromm.de

Eric Fromm Archive
and Literary Estate
Erich Fromm bequeathed the greater part of his library and his scientific work to Rainer Funk and appointed him his literary executor.
A small part is at the New York Public Library in New York City; some of his library remains with the Instituto Mexicano de Psicoanálisis:
C. de Odontologia, 9
Col. Copilco Universidad,
Deleg. Coyoacán,
04360-México,
D. F., México

That part administered by Rainer Funk is kept at the Erich-Fromm-Archiv in Tübingen and is available for scientific research. Contact:
Dr. Rainer Funk, Ursrainer Ring 24
D–72076 Tübingen
Telephone: +49 (0)7071 - 600004
Fax: +49(0)7071 - 600049;
Email: fromm@germanymail.com;

Select Index to the Writings of Erich Fromm

The following index is a selection of those writings that are important for an understanding of Fromm's development and thinking. Titles are printed either in the original language (until 1938 Fromm wrote in German, thereafter in English) or, if present, in their English translation.

An comprehensive, updated index of the works of Erich Fromm, including all translations, is to be found in Vol. 10 of *Erich Fromm Gesamtausgabe in zwölf Bänden* (GA), Stuttgart: Deutsche Verlags-Anstalt, and München: Deutscher Taschenbuch Verlag, 1999.

A grammalogue below indicates the year of first publication and corresponds with the short form within the *Erich Fromm Gesamtausgabe*. Years in square brackets -[ ]- indicate the year of writing of those works, which were published posthumously. Italicized titles are book titles.

1922a et al.: "Ein prinzipielles Wort zur Erziehungsfrage," in: *Jüdische Rundschau*, Frankfurt No. 103/104 (23. 12. 1922).

1922b "Rabbiner Nobel als Führer der Jugend," in: *Neue Jüdische Presse*, Frankfurt am Main (2. 2. 1922), p. 3.

1927a "Der Sabbat," GA VI, pp. 1-9.

1929a "Psychoanalyse und Soziologie," GA I, pp. 3-5; "Psychoanalysis and Sociology," in: S. E. Bronner and D. M. Kellner (Eds.), *Critical Theory and Society. A Reader*, New York and London (Routledge) 1989, pp. 37-39.

1930a "Die Entwicklung des Christusdogmas. Eine psychoanalytische Studie zur sozialpsychologischen Funktion der Religion," GA VI, pp. 11-68; The Dogma of Christ, in: (1963a), pp. 3-91.

1930b "Der Staat als Erzieher. Zur Psychologie der Strafjustiz," GA I, pp. 7-10; The State as Educator, in: Anderson, K., und Quinney, R. (Eds.): *Erich Fromm and Critical Criminology*, Champaign (University of Illinois Press) 2000.

1931a "Zur Psychologie des Verbrechers und der strafenden Gesellschaft," GA I, pp. 11-30; "On the Psychology of the Criminal and the Punitive Society," in: Anderson, K., und Quinney, R. (Eds.): *Erich Fromm and Critical Criminology*, Champaign (University of Illinois Press) 2000.

1931b "Politik und Psychoanalyse," GA I, pp. 31-36; "Politics and Psychoanalysis, Politics and Psychoanalysis," in: S. E. Bronner and D. M. Kellner (Eds.), *Critical Theory and Society. A Reader*, New York and London (Routledge) 1989, pp. 213-18.

1932a "Über Methode und Aufgabe einer Analytischen Sozialpsychologie. Bemerkungen über Psychoanalyse und historischen Materialismus," GA I, pp. 37-57; The Method and Function of an Analytic Social Psychology, in: (1970a), pp. 135-162.

1932b "Die psychoanalytische Charakterologie und ihre Bedeutung für die Sozialpsychologie," GA I, pp. 59-77; "Psychoanalytic Characterology and Its Relevance for Social Psychology," in: (1970a), pp. 163-189.

1933a "Robert Briffaults *Werk über das Mutterrecht*," GA I, pp. 79-84.

1934a "Die sozialpsychologische Bedeutung der Mutterrechtstheorie," GA I, pp. 85-109; "The Theory of Mother Right and Its Relevance for Social Psychology," in: (1970a), pp. 106-134.

1935a "Die gesellschaftliche Bedingtheit der psychoanalytischen Therapie," GA I, pp. 115-138.

1936a "Sozialpsychologischer Teil," GA I, pp. 139-187.

1937a "Zum Gefühl der Ohnmacht," GA I, pp. 189-206.

1939a "The Social Philosophy of 'Will Therapy,'" in: *Psychiatry. Journal for the Study of Interpersonal Process*, Washington (The William Alanson Psychiatric Foundation), Vol. 2 (1939), pp. 229-237.

1939b "Selfishness and Self-Love," in: (1994a), New York (Fromm International Publishing Corporation) 1997, pp. 163-195.

1941a *Escape from Freedom*, New York (Farrar and Rinehart) 1941.

1943b "Sex and Character," in: (1994a), New York (Fromm International Publishing Corporation) 1997, pp. 93-114.

1943c "What Shall We Do With Germany?," in: *Saturday Review of Literature*, New York, Vol. 26 (29.5.1943), pp. 10.

1944a "Individual and Social Origins of Neurosis," in: *American Sociological Review*, New York, Vol. 9 (1944), pp. 380-384.

1947a *Man for Himself. An Inquiry into the Psychology of Ethics*, New York (Rinehart and Co.) 1947.

1949c "Psychoanalytic Characterology and Its Application to the Understanding of Culture," in: S. S. Sargent and M. W. Smith (Eds.): *Culture and Personality*, New York (Viking Press) 1949, pp. 1-12.

1950a *Psychoanalysis dnd Religion*, New Haven (Yale University Press) 1950.

1951a *The Forgotten Language. An Introduction to the Understanding of Dreams, Fairy Tales and Myths*, New York (Rinehart and Co.) 1951.

1951b "Man-Woman," in: M. M. Hughes (Ed.): *The People in Your Life: Psychiatry and Personal Relations*, New York (Alfred A. Knopf) 1951, pp. 3-27.

1955a *The Sane Society,* New York (Rinehart and Winston, Inc.) 1955.

1955c "The Present Human Condition," in: *The American Scholar*, New Haven, Vol. 25 (1955/1956), pp. 29-35.

1955d "Remarks on the Problem of Free Association," in: *Psychiatric Research Report*, Washington (American Psychiatric Association), Vol. 2 (1955), pp. 1-6.

1956a *The Art of Loving. An Inquiry into the Nature of Love*, New York (Harper and Row 1956 and Centennial Edition, Continuum Publishing Company, 2000)

1957a "Man Is Not a Thing," in: *Saturday Review*, New York, Vol. 40 (16.3.1957), pp. 9-11.

1958a "Psychoanalysis-Scientism or Fanaticism?" in: *Saturday Review*, New York, Vol. 41 (14.6.1958), pp. 11-13.55f.

1959a *Sigmund Freud's Mission. An Analysis of His Personality and Influence,* New York (Harper and Row) 1959.

1959c "The Creative Attitude," in: H. A. Anderson (Ed.): *Creavity and Its Cultivation*, New York (Harper and

Row) 1959, pp. 44-54.

1960a "Psychoanalysis and Zen Buddhism," in: D. T. Suzuki and E. Fromm: *Zen Buddhism and Psychoanalysis*, New York (Harper and Row) 1960, pp. 77-141.

1960b *Let Man Prevail-A Socialist Manifesto and Program*, New York (The Call Association) 1960.

1960e Foreword to: A. S. Neill: *Summerhill-A Radical Approach to Child Rearing*, New York (Hart Publishers Co.) 1960, pp. ix-xvi.

1961a *May Man Prevail? An Inquiry into the Facts and Fictions of Foreign Policy*, New York (Doubleday) 1961.

1961b *Marx's Concept of Man*. With a translation of Marx's "Economic and Philosophical Manuscripts" by T. B. Bottomore, New York (F. Ungar Publisher Co.) 1961 and Continuum Publishing Company (1961,1966,1994).

1962a *Beyond the Chains of Illusion. My Encounter with Marx and Freud*, New York (Simon and Schuster) 1962.

1962b and Michael Maccoby: "A Debate on the Question of Civil Defense," in: *Commentary. A Jewish Review*, New York, Vol. 33 (1962), pp. 11-23.

1963a *The Dogma of Christ and Other Essays on Religion, Psychology and Culture*, New York (Holt, Rinehart and Winston) 1963.

1963b "The Revolutionary Character," in (1963a), pp. 103-107.

1963c "Medicine and the Ethical Problem of Modern Man," in (1963a), pp. 118-32.

1963d "Disobedience as a Psychological and Moral Problem," in: Clara Urquart (Ed.): *A Matter of Life*, London (Jonathan Cape) 1963, pp. 97-105.

1963e "C. G. Jung: Prophet of the Unconscious. A Discussion of *Memories, Dreams, Reflexions* by C. G. Jung," in: *Scientific American*, New York (Scientific American Inc.), Vol. 209 (1963), pp. 283-90.

1963f "Humanismo y Psicoanálisis," in: *La Prensa Medica Mexicana*, México, Vol. 28 (1963), pp. 120-26; "Humanism and Psychoanalysis," in: *Contemporary Psychoanalysis*, New York (The Academic Press, Inc.), Vol. 1 (1964), pp. 69-79.

1963g *War Within Man. A Psychological Inquiry into the Roots of Destructiveness. A Study and Commentaries* (Peace Literature Service of the American Friends Service), Philadelphia (American Philadelphia Service Committee) 1963.

1964a *The Heart of Man. Its Genius for Good and Evil*, New York (Harper and Row) 1964.

1965a *Socialist Humanism. An International Symposium*, Ed. Erich Fromm, New York (Doubleday) 1965.

1965c "The Application of Humanist Psychoanalysis to Marx's Theory," in (1965a), pp. 207-22.

1966a *You Shall Be as Gods. A Radical Interpretation of the Old Testament and Its Tradition*, New York (Holt, Rinehart and Winston) 1966.

1966c "The Psychological Aspects of the Guaranteed Income," in: R. Theobald (Ed.): *The Guaranteed Income. Next Step in Economic Evolution?*, New York (Doubleday and Co.) 1966, pp. 175-84.

1966f Interview with Richard Evans: "Dialogue With Erich Fromm," New York (Harper and Row) 1966.

1966k et al.: "El complejo de Edipo: Comentarios al 'Analisis de la fobia de un nino de cinco anos,'" in: *Revista de Psicoanálisis, Psiquiatría y Psicología*, México, No. 4

(1966), pp. 26-33.; "The Oedipus Complex: Comments on 'The Case of Little Hans,'" in: *Contemporary Psychoanalysis*, New York (The Academic Press, Inc.), Vol. 4 (1968), S. 178-188.

1967b "Prophets and Priests," in: R. Schoenman (Ed.): *Bertrand Russell. Philosopher of the Century: Essays in His Honor*, London (George Allen & Unwin) 1967, pp. 67-79.

1968a *The Revolution of Hope. Toward a Humanized Technology*, New York (Harper and Row) 1968.

1968b and Ramón Xirau (Eds.): *The Nature of Man. Readings* selected, edited and furnished with an introduction by Erich Fromm and Ramón Xirau, New York (Macmillan) 1968.

1968g Introduction, to (1968b), pp. 3-24.

1968h "Marx's Contribution to the Knowledge of Man," in: *Social Science Information*, Den Haag, Vol. 7 (1968), pp. 7-17.

1968k et al.: *La sociedad industrial contemporanea*, México (Siglo XXI) 1968.

1970a *The Crisis of Psychoanalysis. Essays on Freud, Marx and Social Psychology*, New York (Holt, Rinehart and Winston) 1970.

1970b and Michael Maccoby: *Social Character in a Mexican Village. A Sociopsychoanalytic Study*, Englewood Cliffs (Prentice Hall) 1970; reprint and with a new introduction by Michael Maccoby, New Brunswick and London (Transaction Publisher) 1996.

1970c "The Crisis of Psychoanalysis," in (1970a), pp. 9-41. .

1970d "Freud's Model of Man and Its Social Determinants," in (1970a), pp. 42-61. .

1970e "Humanistic Planning," in (1970a), pp. 77-87. .

1970f "The Significance of the Theory of Mother Right for Today," in (1970a), pp. 100-105. .

1970g Epilogue to (1970a), pp. 190-192. .

1970h "Zur Theorie und Strategie des Friedens," GA V, pp. 243-257.

1970i Essay in: *Summerhill: For and Against*, New York (Hart Publishing Company) 1970, pp. 251-263.

1970n et al.: *La Familia*, introducción de Ralph Linton, Barcelona (ediciones península) 1970.

1972a "Der Traum ist die Sprache des universalen Menschen," GA IX, pp. 311-15; "Dreams Are the Universal Language of Man," in: (1983a), pp. 39-58.

1972b "Einige post-marxsche und post-freudsche Gedanken über Religion und Religiosität," GA VI, S. 293-299; "Some Post-Marxian and Post-Freudian Thoughts on Religion and Religiousness," in: *Concilium*, Nijmegen (Stichting Concilium), Vol. 8 (1972), pp. 146-54.

1972c "The Erich Fromm Theory of Aggression," in: *The New York Times Magazine*, New York (27.2.1972), pp. 14f.71.76.80f.84 and 86.

1973a *The Anatomy of Human Destructiveness*, New York (Holt, Rinehart and Winston) 1973.

1974a "Psychologie für Nichtpsychologen," GA VIII, pp. 71-90; "Psychology for Nonpsychologists," in: (1983a), pp. 66-8.

1974b "Im Namen des Lebens," GA XI; "In the Name of Life. A Portrait through Dialogue," in: (1983a), pp. 88-116.

1974c "Hitler-wer war er und was heißt Widerstand gegen diesen Menschen. Interview mit Hans Jürgen

Schultz," GA XI; "Hitler-Who Was He and What Constituted Resistance Against Him?" in: (1983a), pp. 117-133.

1975b   "Interview with Adelbert Reif: *Aggression Und Charakter*," Zürich (Verlag die Arche) 1975.

1976a   *To Have Or to Be?* New York (Harper and Row 1976 and Continuum Publishing Company, 1995, 1996).

1976g   *Critica de la sexualidad y la familia* (Antigua casa editorial No. 10), Buenos Aires (Cuervo) 1976.

1977g   Das psychoanalytische Bild vom Menschen und seine gesellschaftliche Standortbedingtheit, GA VIII, pp. 243-51.

1979a   *Greatness and Limitations of Freud's Thought*, New York (Harper and Row) 1980.

1980a   *Arbeiter ind Angestellte am Vorabend des Dritten Reiches. Eine sozialpsychologische Untersuchung*, Stuttgart (Deutsche Verlags-Anstalt) 1980; *The Working Class in Weimar Germany. A Psychological and Sociological Study*, edited and introduced by Wolfgang Bonß, London (Berg Publishers) 1984.

1980e   Interview with Guido Ferrari: *Erich Fromm, Il coraggio di essere*, Bellinzona (Edizione Casagrande) 1980.

1981a   *On Disobedience and Other Essays*, New York (The Seabury Press) 1981.

1983a   *Über die Liebe zum Leben. Rundfunksendungen* edited by Hans Jürgen Schultz, Stuttgart (Deutsche Verlags-Anstalt) 1983; *For the Love of Life,* Ed. Hans Jürgen Schultz, New York (The Free Press, Macmillan) 1986.

1983b   "Überfluß und Überdruß in unserer Gesellschaft," GA XI; "Affluence and Ennui in Our Society," in: (1983a), pp. 1-38.

1983c   "Über die Ursprünge der Aggression," GA XI; On the Origins of Aggression, in: (1983a), pp. 39-58.

1985a   *Erich-Fromm-Lesebuch*, Stuttgart (Deutsche Verlags-Anstalt) 1985; *The Erich Fromm Reader*. Readings Selected and Edited by Rainer Funk. Foreword by Joel Kovel, New Jersey (Humanities Press) 1994.

1989a   *The Art of Being*, edited by Rainer Funk, New York (Continuum Publishing Company) 1993.

1989b   [1922] *Das Jüdische Gesetz. Zur Soziologie des Diasporaentums. Dissertation von 1922*, Ed. R. Funk. Weinheim/Basel (Beltz Verlag) 1989; GA XI.

1989c   *Schriften über Sigmund Freud*, ausgewählt und eingeleitet von Rainer Funk, Stuttgart (Deutsche Verlags-Anstalt) 1989.

1990a   *The Revision of Psychoanalysis*, Boulder (Westview Press) 1992.

1990b   *Ethik und Politiik. Antworten auf aktuelle politische Fragen*, Ed. Rainer Funk, Weinheim/Basel (Beltz Verlag) 1990.

1990c   *Wege zur Befreiung. Über die Kunst des Lebens*, ausgewählt und mit einem Vorwort von Rainer Funk, Zürich (Manesse Verlag) 1990.

1990d   [1969] "On My Psychoanalytic Approach," in (1990a), pp. 1-9.

1990e   [1969] "The Necessity for the Revision of Psychoanalysis," in (1990a), pp. 11-19.

1990f   [1969] "The Dialectic Revision of Psychoanalysis," in (1990a), pp. 19-80.

1990g   [1969] "Sexuality and Sexual Perversions," in (1990a), pp. 81-110.

1990h   [1968] "The Alleged Radicalism of Herbert Marcuse," in (1990a), pp. 111-29.

1991a   *The Art of Listening*. Edited and with a Foreword by Rainer Funk, New York (Continuum Publishing Company) 1994.

1991b   *Die Pathologie der Normalität. Zur Wissenschaft vom Menschen*, Weinheim/Basel (Beltz Verlag) 1991.

1991c   [1964] "Factors Leading to Patient's Change in Analytic Treatment," in (1991a), pp. 15-41.

1991d   [1974] "Therapeutic Aspects of Psychoanalysis," in (1991a), pp. 45-193.

1991e   [1953] "Die Pathologie der Normalität des heutigen Menschen," GA XI.

1991h   [1974] "Ist der Mensch von Natur aus faul?" GA XII.

1992a   *Gesellschaft und Seele. Beiträge zur Sozialpsychologie und zur psychoanalytischen Praxis*, Weinheim/Basel (Beltz Verlag) 1992.

1992b   *On Being Human*. Foreword by Rainer Funk, New York (Continuum Publishing Company) 1994.

1992c   *Worte Wie Wege*, published and initiated by Rainer Funk, Freiburg, Basel, Wien (Herder Verlag) 1992.

1992d   [1937] "Die Determiniertheit der psychischen Struktur durch die Gesellschaft. Zur Methode und Aufgabe einer Analytischen Sozialpsychologie," GA XI.

1992e   [1959] "Das Unbewußte und die psychoanalytische Praxis ," (3 lectures), GA XII.

1992k   [1969] "The Disintegration of Societies," in (1992b), pp. 41-50.

1992m   [1962] "A New Humanism as a Condition for the One World," in (1992b), pp. 61-79.

1992r   [1978] "Remarks on the Relations between Germans and Jews," in (1992b), pp. 105-10.

1992s   [1974] "Meister Eckhart and Karl Marx on Having and Being," in (1992b), pp. 114-70.

1993a   *Die Gesellschaft als Gegenstand der Psychoanalyse. Frühe Schriften zur Analytischen Sozialpsychologie*, Ed. Rainer Funk, Frankfurt (Suhrkamp) 1993.

1993b   *The Essential Fromm: Life between Having and Being*, New York (Continuum Publishing Company) 1995.

1993c   [1974] "On the Art of Living," in (1993b), pp. 15-19.

1994a   *Love, Sexuality, and Matriarchy. About Gender*, Ed. and with an introduction by Rainer Funk, New York (Fromm International Publishing Corporation) 1997.

1994b   [1955] "Bachofen's Discovery of the Mother Right, in: (1994a), pp. 3-18.

1994c   [1933] "Die männliche Schöpfung," GA XI; "The Male Creation," in: (1994a), pp 46-75.

1994d   [1940] "Changing Concepts of Homosexuality," in: (1994a), pp. 148-161.

Select writings on Erich Fromm

The following list is only a small selection of publications that deal directly with the thinking and works of Erich Fromm. The international bibliography with almost 4,000 titles can be bought from the Erich Fromm Archive (Ursrainer Ring 24, D-72076 Tübingen, Fax: +49-7071-600049); Except for the abstracts, it is also available in the website of the Erich Fromm Archive at: www.erich-fromm.de.

Anderson, K. and Quinney, R. (eds.) 2000: *Erich Fromm and Critical Criminology*, Champaign (University of Illinois Press).

Bierhoff, B.,1991: *Erich Fromm. Analytische Sozialpsychologie und visionäre Gesellschaftskritik*, Opladen (Westdeutscher Verlag).

Burston, D. 1991: *The Legacy of Erich Fromm*, Cambridge (Mass.) and London (Harvard University Press).

Classen, J. (ed.) 1987: *Erich Fromm und die Pädagogik. Gesellschafts-Charakter und Erziehung*, Weinheim/Basel (Beltz Verlag).

Classen, J. (ed.) 1991: *Erich Fromm und die Kritische Pädagogik*, Weinheim/Basel (Beltz Verlag).

Cortina, M., and Maccoby, M. (eds.) 1996: *A Prophetic Analyst. Erich Fromm's Contribution to Psychoanalysis*, Nothvale and London (Jason Aronson Inc.).

Cusimano, F. A., and Luban-Plozza, B. 1984: *Erich Fromm*, Milano (Pileio Edizioni).

Eletti, P. L. (ed.) 1988: *Incontro con Erich Fromm*. Atti del Simposio Internazionale su Erich Fromm: "Dalla necrofilia alla biofilia: linee per una psicoanalisi umanistica," Firenze 1986, Firenze (Edizioni Medicea).

Frederking, V. 1994: *Durchbruch vom Haben zum Sein. Erich Fromm und die Mystik Meister Eckharts*, with an appendix "Unveröffentlichte Fragmente Erich Fromms," Paderborn (Ferdinand Schöningh).

Funk, R. 1978: *Mut zum Menschen. Erich Fromms Denken und Werk, seine humanistische Religion und Ethik*, Stuttgart (Deutsche Verlags-Anstalt).

Funk, R. 1983: *Erich Fromm*. Mit Selbstzeugnissen und Bilddokumenten, Hamburg (Rowohlts Bildmonographien 322).

Funk, R., Johach, H. and Meyer, G., 2000: *Erich Fromm heute. Zur Aktualität seines Denkens*, München (Deutscher Taschenbuch Verlag).

Görlich, B. (ed.) 1980: *Der Stachel Freud. Beiträge und Dokumente zur Kulturismuskritik*, Frankfurt (Suhrkamp).

Hardeck, J. 1992: *Vernunft und Liebe*, Berlin (Ullstein Sachbuch 34933).

Hausdorff, D. 1972: *Erich Fromm*, New York (Twayne Publishers).

Internationale Erich-Fromm-Gesellschaft (ed.): *Wissenschaft vom Menschen / Science of Man*. Jahrbuch der Internationalen Erich-Fromm-Gesellschaft, Münster (Lit Verlag). Vols I to VI (1990-1995); Continued: *Fromm Forum*, Tübingen (Selbstverlag) No 1 (1997) to 4 (2000).

Internationale Erich-Fromm-Gesellschaft (ed.), 1995: *Die Charaktermauer. Zur Psychoanalyse des Gesellschafts-Charakters in Ost- und Westdeutschland*, Göttingen (Vandenhoeck & Ruprecht).

Kessler, M. and Funk, R. (eds.): *Erich Fromm und die Frankfurter Schule*, Tübingen (Francke Verlag).

Klein, E. 1987: *Die Theorie des Subjekts bei Erich Fromm*, Frankfurt/New York (Campus).

Knapp, G. P. 1988: *Erich Fromm* Berlin (Colloquium Verlag).

Knapp, G. P. 1989: *The Art of Living. Erich Fromm's Life and Works*, New York (Peter Lang).

Lundgren, S. 1998: *Fight Against Idols. Erich Fromm on Religion, Judaism and the Bible*, Frankfurt (Peter Lang).

Millán, S. and Gojman de Millán, S., 1981: *Erich Fromm y el psicoanálisis humanista*, México (Siglo XXI).

Saciuk, R. 1996: *O Moralnosci i zdrowiu psychiczbyn, Z humanistycznej psychoanalizy E. Fromma*, Wroclaw (Wydawnictwo Uniwersytetu Wroclawskiego).

Schaar, J. H., 1961: *Escape from Authority. The Perspectives of Erich Fromm*, New York (Harper and Row) .

Tauscher, P. 1985: *Nekrophilie und Faschismus*. Erich Fromm's contribution on the sociobiographical interpretation of Adolf Hitler and further sociopsychological interpretations. Frankfurt (Haag + Herchen).

Wehr, H. 1989: *Das Subjektmodell der Kritischen Theorie Erich Fromms als Leitbild humanistischen pädagogischen Handelns*, Frankfurt (Verlag Peter Lang).

Wehr, H., 1990: *Erich Fromm zur Einführung*, Hamburg (Junius Verlag).

Werder, L. von (ed.),1987: *Der unbekannte Fromm. Biographische Studien*, Frankfurt (Haag + Herchen).

Important dates in the life of Erich Fromm

1900   23rd March: Born Erich Pinchas Fromm in Frankfurt am Main. Only child of the Orthodox Jewish wine trader, Naphtali Fromm and his wife Rosa, née Krause.

1918   Final exam at Wöhler-Schule in Frankfurt, then two semesters studying jurisprudence at the University of Frankfurt. Friendship with Rabbi Nehemia Nobel.

1919   Cofounder of the Freie Jüdische Lehrhaus (Free Jewish Teaching Institute) in Frankfurt am Main. Student in Heidelberg from the summer semester onwards.

1920   At Heidelberg, he switches from studying jurisprudence to sociology and national economy under Alfred Weber. Until 1925, he continues Talmudic studies with Rabbi Rabinkow.

1922   Receives his doctorate in sociology from Heidelberg.

1924   Together with Frieda Reichmann, opens the *Therapeutikum* in Mönchhofstrasse, Heidelberg. Psychoanalysed by Frieda Reichmann, later by Wilhelm Wittenberg in Munich.

1926   16th June: Marries Frieda Reichmann. Turns away from Orthodox Judaism. Contacts with Georg Groddeck in Baden Baden.

1927   First publications as an orthodox Freudian.

1928   Educational analysis with Hanns Sachs in Berlin and psychonanalytical studies at the Karl Abraham Institute in Berlin.

1929   Co-founder of the South German Institute for Psychoanalysis in Frankfurt, together with Karl Landauer, Frieda Fromm-Reichmann and Heinrich Meng.

1930   Member of the Institute for Social Research in Frankfurt, in charge of the fields of psychoanalysis and social psychology. Completes his his psychoanalytic training in Berlin and opens his own practice there.

1931   Falls ill with tuberculosis of the lungs during the summer. Separation from Frieda Fromm-Reichmann. Stays on and off in Davos until April 1934.

1932   Publication of the article "Über Methode und Aufgabe einer analytischen Sozialpsychologie" (The Method and Function of an Analytical Social Psychology) in the first edition of the *Zeitschrift für Sozialforschung (Studies in Philosophies and Social Sciences)*.

1933   At the invitation of Karen Horney, guest lectures in Chicago. Works on the theory of matriarchal systems. Death of his father. Friendship with Karen Horney (lasts until 1943).

1934   25th May: Emigrates to the U.S.A., arriving in New York on the 31st of May, 1934. Works at the Institute for Social Research until 1939, repeatedly interrupted by health problems. Evaluation of his 1930 social-psychological studies of German workers and employees.

1935   Publication of the article "Die gesellschaftliche Bedingtheit der psychoanalytischen Therapie" (The Social Determination of Psychoanalytic Therapy). Cooperation with Harry Stack Sullivan and Clara Thompson. Frieda Fromm-Reichmann goes to Chestnut Lodge near Washington DC.

1936   Publication of his concept of the authoritarian character in Horkheimer's *Studien über Autorität und Familie (Studies in Authority and the Family)*.

1937   Revision of his psychoanalytical approach: psychoanalysis as analytical social psychology (relationship theory versus drive theory). Rejection of his revision of the Freudian drive-theory by Horkheimer, Löwenthal, Marcuse and Adorno.

1938   During his stay in Europe, a new outbreak of his tuberculosis. Six months' convalescence on the Schatzalp above Davos.

1939   Parted with the Institute for Social Research. First Publication in English.

1940   25th May: American citizenship

1941   Publishes *Escape from Freedom* and begins teaching at the New School for Social Research in New York.

1942   Part-time professorship at Bennington College, Vermont.

1943   Breaks with Horney. Foundation of the William Alanson White Institute in New York.

1944   24th July: Marriage to Henny Gurland.

1947   Publication of *Man for Himself* which includes his concept of the marketing character orientation.

1948   Terry Lecturer at Yale University on Psychoanalysis and Religion. (Eponymous book published in 1950). Henny Gurland falls ill.

1950   6th June: Moves to Mexico City.

1951   Professor extraordinary at the Medical Faculty of the National Autonomous University of Mexico. First course with students of psychoanalysis. (Remains in Mexico until 1974).

1952   4th June: Henny Gurland-Fromm dies.

1953   18th December: Marriage to Annis Freeman, née Glover.

1955   Publication of *The Sane Society* containing an argument for a communitarian socialism.

1956   Publication of the world bestseller, *The Art of Loving*. (Continuum International) 2000. Foundation of a Mexican psychoanalytic society. Moves from Mexico City to Cuernavaca.

1957   Seminar with Daisetz T. Suzuki. Death of Frieda Fromm-Reichmann. First preparations for socio-psychological field research among Mexican peasants.

1959   Death of his mother in New York. She had lived there since 1941. Publication of the book *Sigmund Freud's Mission. An Analysis of his Personality and Influence.*

1960   Intensified political engagement for the Socialist Party of the U.S.A. More lecturing in the U.S.A.

1961   Publication of *Marx's Concept of Man* and a work on American foreign policy.

1962   Peace conference in Moscow. Foundation of the IFPS (umbrella organisation of non-orthodox psychoanalytical societies). Publication of *Beyond the Chains of Illusion*.

1963   Opening of the Mexican Psychoanalytical Institute.

1964   Publication of his biophilia–necrophilia concept, as well as the the application of narcissism to societal groups in *The Heart of Man*.

Image Acknowledgments

1965 Emeritus status at the National Autonomous University of Mexico. Greater engagement in peace politics and against the Vietnam war. Height of his fame in the U.S.A.

1966 Publication of *You Shall be as Gods*. A heart attack leads to his retreat from active duties in Mexico. Stays in Europe for long periods.

1968 Assists in the presidential election campain of Eugene McCarthy and publishes *The Revolution of Hope*. After Nixon's victory, withdraws from political activism. Starts work on his theory of aggression.

1969 Rents an apartment in Locarno, Ticino, Southern Switzerland, as a summer retreat.

1970 Publication of his field-research on Mexican peasants.

1973 Publication of *The Anatomy of Human Destructiveness*.

1974 Decides to give up the house in Cuernavaca and to stay in Ticino all year round.

1975 Writing *To Have Or to Be?* Gall bladder operation in New York.

1976 Publication of *To Have Or to Be?*

1977 Second heart attack. Fromm becomes a leading figure of the alternative movement in Germany and Italy.

1978 Third heart attack brings on a deterioration of his condition.

1980 18th March: Dies as a result of a fourth heart attack. Cremation in Bellinzona, Switzerland.

Unless otherwise mentioned, rights for the photographs and copies of documents reside with:

Dr. Rainer Funk
Ursrainer Ring 24
D-72076 Tübingen
Telephone: +49 7071 6000 04
Fax: +49 7071 6000 49
E-mail: fromm@germanymail.com

Albert Schweizer Cahiers: p. 150
Anders, Hans-Jörg, STERN Syndication: pp. 157, 158, 159, 160, 161.
Bamberger, Naftali Bar-Giora: p. 9 (gravestones).
Bild der Wissenschaft (DVA): p. 156; (Back of envelope)
Delakova, Katya: p. 163
Foerg, Irmgard: p. 162 (Kreutzberger)
Frankfurter Stadtarchiv: p. 35 (Wöhler-Gymnasium)
Freud Museum, London: pp. 61, 65 (Ferenczi), 67, 70, 111, 112
Goldmann, Thea: p. 165 (Envelope)
Horney, Marianne: pp. 65, 116
Internationaler Psychoanalytischer Verlag: p. 63 (*The Soul Searcher*)
Jüdisches Museum, Frankfurt: pp. 37, 38, 39 (Simon), 40, 41
Kloska, Almuth: p. 135
Krug, Philipp: p. 35 (School play)
Landauer, Eva: p. 73 (Landauer)
Landis, Bernard: p. 163
Leo Baeck Institute, Jerusalem: p. 54 (Rabinkow)
Liebermann, Max: p. 39 (Cohen)
Luban-Plozza, Boris: p. 162 (Luban), 163 (Zander, Illich)
Max-Horkheimer-Archiv, Frankfurt: pp. 72, 73, 80 (Institute building), 83, 88, 89 (Marcuse), 91, 93, 94
Nationalarchiv, Marbach: pp. 62, 63 (Groddeck)
Oncken Verlag: p. 162 (Nyanaponica)
Oswaldo, Excelsior (Mexico): p. 153
Preussischer Kulturbesitz: p 69
Silva, Jorge: pp. 131, 134, 141 (Valesco)
Storch, Werner: p. 86
Universal: p. 99 (Cartoon, 1969)
Universitätsarchiv, Heidelberg: p. 53 (Weber)
Will, Herbert: p. 112 (Groddeck)
William Alanson White Institute, New York: pp. 107, 113, 117, 129

Index of names